atil4 5B

worship:

beyond inculturation

worship:

beyond
inculturation

Anscar J. **chupungco**, OSB

The Pastoral Press
Washington, DC

ISBN: 1-56929-018-0

The Pastoral Press
225 Sheridan Street, N.W.
Washington, D.C. 20011
(202) 723-1254

The Pastoral Press is the publications division of the National Association of Pastoral Musicians, a membership organization of musicians
and clergy dedicated to fostering the art of musical liturgy.

Printed in the United States of America

Contents

Preface

The subtitle of this book was inspired by Vatican II's Constitution on the Liturgy: "That sound tradition may be retained and yet the way remain open to legitimate progress, a careful investigation is always to be made into each part of the liturgy to be revised" (art. 23). Tradition and progress are the two essential components of liturgical renewal. If the church's worship is to remain contemporary, it must be constantly renewed like the ecclesial life, mission, and theology of which it is the chief expression. Yet we know that liturgical renewal does not come out of the blue, nor does it spring up from the ground with the rapid growth of mushrooms. The church has been around for twenty centuries; it has roots deeply embedded in history and has a long memory of things. This is why true renewal can happen only in the context of tradition. What the Rule of St. Benedict, chapter 64, requires of the abbot of a monastery can be required of today's liturgist: "to have a treasury of knowledge from which to bring out what is new and what is old (Mt 13:52)." Liturgical renewal is both faithful continuity with the past and courageous thrust into the future.

This book gathers nine papers and articles I have written on liturgical history and renewal, with focus on inculturation. Each is presented as a chapter. The first four deal with historical questions, while the next four with issues pertaining to continuing renewal, especially of the order of Mass. The last serves as epilogue. Chapters One, Two, and Four: "The Early Cultural

Setting of the Baptismal Liturgy," "The Cultural and Domestic Traditions of the Eucharist," and "Liturgical Music and Its Cultural Setting," are unpublished papers I read at the Consultation on Worship and Culture organized by the Lutheran World Federation in Cartigny, Switzerland, in October 1993. Chapter Five, "Tradition and Progress: The Order of Mass Revisited" is also an unpublished paper I read at the annual meeting of the Federation of Diocesan Liturgical Commissions held in Miami, Florida, in October 1992. Chapter Eight, "Liturgical Pluralism in Multiethnic Communities," is a revised version of my paper for the Regional Meeting of the National Association of Pastoral Musicians held in Nassau, Bahamas, in September 1992. The original text appeared in *Pastoral Music* (February-March 1993) pp. 28-35. All these papers have undergone significant revision and rewriting. Chapter Six, "Toward a Ferial Order of Mass" appeared in *Ecclesia Orans* 10:1 (1993) pp. 11-32. Chapter Nine, "History and Culture in the Study of Liturgy" is a total revision of an older material published in *Seminarium* 2-3 (1985) pp. 256-65. Chapter Three, "The Early Cultural Setting of Ordination Rites," and Chapter Seven, "The Shaping of the Filipino Order of Mass," are new material.

I am grateful to all who assisted me in my work: my colleagues at the Pontifical Liturgical Institute in Rome, especially Prof. Michael Witczak who patiently checked some of my bibliographical references; Rev. S. Anita Stauffer who encouraged me to delve into areas of historical studies with which I was not quite familiar; the staff and students of Paul VI Institute of Liturgy in the Philippines who journeyed with me in my search for a ferial order of Mass; and all those who contributed to the shaping of the Filipino Order of Mass, especially my former students at Maryhill School of Theology in the Philippines. A word of thanks goes to Mr. Lawrence Johnson of The Pastoral Press, who thought that this collection of papers and articles was worth putting into a book.

Anscar J. Chupungco, OSB

1

The Early Cultural Setting of the Baptismal Liturgy

ONE OF THE REMARKABLE TRAITS OF THE GRECO-ROMAN PERIOD OF THE church, especially during the third and fourth centuries, was the rapid development of the shape of liturgical worship. Stepping out of the Jewish world, the young missionary church entered into contact with the culture and cultic practices of pagan Greece and Rome. Considering the staunch monotheism inherited by the church from Judaism, contact with the pagan world entailed a considerable effort to adapt to the new situation without detriment to the church's basic tenets. This is not to say that the church had no previous experience in this matter. The dream of Peter in the city of Joppa (Acts 11:4-18), the council of the Apostles in Jerusalem (Acts 15:4-29), and the entire apostolic activity of Paul to the gentile world bear witness to the early church's struggle to grapple with problems arising from contact with paganism or with cultures outside Judaism.

Yet the experience of the church in the third and fourth centuries had a different tenor from the apostolic period. It was not a question merely of admitting the gentiles into the church and exempting them from some of the mosaic laws that still bound Christians; rather it was a question of investing the Christian rites of worship with elements from the culture and traditions of the gentiles. It was an altogether different process to which we give the name of inculturation. We may say that inculturation at this early stage of liturgical development became a distinct liturgical concern of the young missionary church.

1

What led the church to inculturate its form of worship, and how did the church do it? The church could have continued to celebrate baptism in the utter New Testament simplicity of "washing in water with the word," using perhaps the language of Palestine. But it did not, nor did the church settle with merely delivering catechetical instruction to converts, as did the missionaries in China in the seventeenth century. In their antagonism to native Chinese words and rites the missionaries foisted Latin words like *Deus* and *gratia* on their converts for whom such words meant absolutely nothing. Furthermore, they forbade them to perform the rite of ancestral veneration, a rite which was and continues to be the mainstay of Chinese civilization. China was lost to the church because at that moment in history the church did not know how to bend to the inevitable. The history of inculturation certainly signals the danger of eclecticism and even syncretism. But it also warns us that when we ignore the relationship worship should have with culture, we might also come to ignore the dynamics of evangelization.

The early church, on the other hand, not only catechized; it also made necessary adjustments in its liturgical rites. If the liturgy must communicate the church's faith to people, it had to be expressed with words, rites, and symbols that were familiar to them. It had to become recognizably incarnate, that is, as having taken flesh in the cultural milieu of the worshipers. Furthermore, it must allow itself to be claimed and owned by them as part and parcel of their existence as a Christian people. It does not mean that inculturation reduces the liturgy to becoming a component of culture. For the core of the liturgy is a supracultural reality which the church received through apostolic preaching and preserves intact in every time and place. What inculturation means is that worship assimilates the people's language, ritual, and symbolic patterns. In this way they are able to claim and own the liturgical core they received through the apostolic preaching. Today we have come to regard both the process of inculturation and the claiming of the Christian message by the people as an imperative to evangelization.

The question that interests us here is how the early church inculturated worship. What method did it employ, so that inculturation did not become an occasion for eclecticism? We know what eclecticism is all about: it is a random, indiscriminate, and undigested borrowing of alien doctrines and practices regardless of whether or not they accord with the faith received from the Apostles. What eclecticism tries to accomplish is to present to the faithful a kind of a multiple choice whereby each one may select elements that one finds suitable or convenient. Christianity detests every form of eclecticism. It is by nature partial to the assimilation in liturgical worship of those cultural elements and patterns which can be reinterpreted in the light of God's revelation. This process of reinterpreting or rereading culture in the light of the Christian mystery is a method of inculturation employed by the early church. In other words, inculturation does not lead to a juxtaposition of unrelated elements. Rather, it allows the liturgy to develop its shape in the cultural milieu of worshipers, without danger to its original meaning.

Because Christianity detests eclecticism, it views culture with a critical eye. Today we speak of this as being countercultural. In the area of the liturgy the church not only welcomes culture; it also critiques culture. The church realizes that while every culture possesses beauty and nobility, not everything it owns can be assimilated into its liturgical worship. In this connection, being countercultural can mean one of three things. The church can ignore what it considers unsuitable or, to put it more strongly, unredeemable. Its silent reproach is one way of being countercultural. Thus the slaughtering of sacrificial animals in some mystery rites as part of initiation process was neither assimilated by nor spoken of in the early rite of Christian baptism. The second way of being countercultural is by denunciation or protest. Early patristic writings, as we shall see, did not spare such pagan initiation rites as lustrations, pomps, and meals. These were ineffective, costly, or even devilish. The third way of being countercultural is by the reinterpretation of cultural elements, including religious rites, in the light of God's revelation. This method, which requires a critique of the value and suitability of cultural components previous to their assimilation, affirms that culture and traditions can serve as vehicles of the Christian mystery. We may say that they enter the realm of Christ's redemption through the liturgy.

BAPTISMAL ELEMENTS IN THE FIRST TWO CENTURIES

The cultural setting of the first two centuries has left an indelible impression on the shape of baptismal liturgy. To appreciate this point it is helpful to recall that in the New Testament the celebration of baptism centered on the bare essentials. Ephesians 5:26 mentions only the "washing of water with the word." On the other hand, the references in Romans 6:4 ("when we were baptized we went into the tomb with him") and Acts 8:38 ("Philip and the eunuch went down into the water") seem to imply the rite of immersion. At any rate, washing or bathing and the word or some ritual formula would appear to have made up the core or nucleus of the New Testament baptismal rite. Throughout the centuries the church has maintained that the baptism of Jesus consisted basically of the act of washing in natural water accompanied by an invocation of the name of the Blessed Trinity, as Matthew 28:19 indicates. In fact, in cases of emergency all the church requires is the washing with water and the recitation of the trinitarian formula, or in other words, the bare essentials of the New Testament baptismal liturgy.

Around the year 90 A.D. the author of the *Didaché* informs us that baptism was administered "in the name of the Father, and of the Son, and of the Holy Spirit."[1] Whether this was the actual formula or was meant to define the trinitarian character of baptism as presented by Matthew 28:19 is difficult to determine. All that we are allowed to conclude is that the three Names were invoked at baptism. Later patristic writings mention the use of the more elaborate credal formula. Thus, in the third-century *Apostolic Tradition* attributed to Hippolytus of Rome the formula is in the form of question and answer before each of the three-fold immersions: "Do you believe in God, the Father almighty? I believe. Do you believe in Jesus Christ, the Son of God, who was born by the Holy Spirit and the Virgin Mary, was crucified under Pontius Pilate, died, was buried, and on the third day rose from the dead, ascended to heaven, sits at the right hand of the Father, and will come to judge both the living and the dead? I believe. Do you believe in the Holy Spirit, the holy Church, and the resurrection of the body? I believe."[2]

As regards the baptismal water, the *Didaché* mentions living, that is, the running water of springs and rivers, or if this is not available, also such bodies of water as pools and reservoirs where water does not flow. Are we to perceive here an early preoccupation for the symbolism of baptismal water as life-giving water? It is evident that the mode of washing was immersion, or was it submersion? The practice of baptism by immersion is confirmed by a later interpolation to the text which directs the baptizer to "pour water three times on the head," in case water was scarce in the region. Thus the rite of infusion would appear to have been rather exceptional. We have here an example of ritual adjustment that laid aside the original meaning of *baptein* or *baptizein* as immersion-bath in view of a concrete situation.

The *Didaché* enjoins both the baptizer and the baptizand to fast for a day or two before the rite of baptism.[3] Fasting before initiation was an element of the ancient nature rites that developed in the third century as mystery rites. It was a form of ascetical preparation for the initiation rites and may be considered a component of the religious cultural milieu of the early centuries. Although no less than the New Testament itself praised the practice of fasting (Mt 6:17; 17:20; Lk 2:37), we have no evidence that fasting was observed in connection with baptism. Hence it would appear that the practice of fasting prior to baptism was borrowed from the religious cultural setting of the time. Since the *Didaché* is a first-century document, its point of reference would seem to be the ancient nature rites before they developed into mystery rites.

We must presume that some kind of catechesis was given to the candidates.[4] Baptisms in Acts were normally preceded by instruction on the faith. We need only think of the grand baptisms on Pentecost, the baptism of the eunuch, and the baptism of the jailer at Philippi. These were preceded by instruction on the Christian faith, which surely included moral or ethical norms, similar to what other religions would require an initiate to know. We may presume that the candidates were required to learn also sacred formulas by heart. One likely example is the Lord's Prayer which is recorded for the first time outside the New Testament by the *Didaché*. Since the *Didaché* requires that the Lord's Prayer be recited three times a day, we may conclude that those initiated into faith had to learn it by heart. Learning sacred formulas was a standard preparation for initiation.

Thus until the end of the first Christian century the rite of baptism was confined to the essentials, namely immersion in water accompanied by the recitation of the trinitarian formula. In the *Didaché* the core of the baptismal liturgy retained the original simplicity of the apostolic rite, yet marginal elements borrowed from the cultural setting of the period began to accrue. In the *Didaché* these are catechesis, which was normally required by the sacrament, and fasting. Today we call such accrued elements introductory, explanatory, or concluding rites.

The influence of the pagan mystery rites can be felt more strongly in the writing of Justin Martyr. Justin wrote his *First Apology*, whose Chapter 61 describes baptism, between the years 148 and 161.[5] Of particular interest to the historical development of the baptismal rite is the mention of the trinitarian formula: "There is invoked over the one who wishes to be reborn and who has repented of one's sins, the name of God, the Father and Master of all . . . Furthermore, the one being illuminated is washed also in the name of Jesus Christ, who was crucified under Pontius Pilate, and in the name of the Holy Spirit who predicted through the prophets everything concerning Jesus."[6] These words ring a familiar bell: they are quite similar to the trinitarian components of the Christian creed. Can we say that in the second century the baptismal formula was already as elaborate as the creed or at least contained a number of credal elements?

Justin, who studied philosophy under the Stoics and later the Platonists, was also conversant with mystery rites. It might be useful to note in passing that mystery rites seem to have originated from nature rites which formerly were performed to renew the fertility of mother earth. Although mystery rites always alluded to one or another natural element like water, fire, and wind, they also included initiation into the community of believers. Until the fourth century, when these rites began to wane, the more common examples were: the Eleusinian rites which honored the bereavement and reunion of the corn-goddess Demeter with her daughter Persephone; the cult of the Egyptian Osiris and Isis featuring the water of the Nile; the Phrygian fertility rites in honor of mother earth and Attis; the Assyrian rites for Juno which centered on the element of air; and the initiation rites which featured the Persian god Mithras and the sun-god.[7]

Justin's description of baptism is evocative of the pagan mystery rites of initiation. He mentions a type of scrutinies, whereby the candidates pledged to live according to "what we say and teach." He informs us that candidates "are taught in prayer and fasting to ask God to forgive their past sins, while we all pray and fast with them." He refers to baptism as *photismos*, or enlightenment, and the baptized as the enlightened ones. It is called so, "because it enlightens the intelligence of those who learn these things".[8] Although the baptismal hymn in Ephesians 5:14 speaks of Christ as one who shines on those who are awakened from sleep, we cannot exclude the possibility that Justin borrowed the word *photismos* directly from the mystery rites. Here we have a remarkable example of how the anthropological axiom "water illumines, while fire washes" is put to work in baptism. The water of baptism not only washes, it also enlightens. Similarly, words like consecration and rebirth, which Justin employs to describe the effects of baptism, were also in use among the different mystery rites.

Initiation meals were part of many mystery rites. Justin could have regarded the first eucharist of the neophytes as the Christian counterpart of such meals. In Chapter 65 of his book the eucharistic celebration appears as the conclusion of the initiatory rite of baptism. It begins with what we know today as general intercessions which follow baptism. Justin's reference to the Mithraic meal reveals the connection he makes between the initiatory rite and the meal. He notes that the Mithraic initiation rite also includes a meal with water and bread, but he claims with typical early Christian disdain that this is a falsification of the eucharist fabricated by the devil, surely in order to sow confusion among Christian believers.[9]

Since baptism was regarded as an initiatory rite, it was to be expected that both the language and the symbols of the prevalent mystery rites, which were initiatory by nature, would eventually creep into the Christian rite. Thus at an early stage the shape of baptism was influenced by this type of religious culture. For the sake of historical accuracy it is necessary to add here that while the church during these centuries welcomed elements of mystery rites, it absolutely condemned idol worship and refrained from the use of anything that had to do with such worship: temples, use of incense and candles, and *pompae* or the ornate carriages of idols. Descending from the monotheistic tradition of Judaism, the church had a physical aversion for such things; it regarded them as devil worship. Not so those elements of pagan initiation rites which could shed light on the meaning of baptism and clearly indicate it to people as the Christian counterpart of pagan initiation rites.

BAPTISMAL ELEMENTS IN THE THIRD
AND FOURTH CENTURIES

In the third century more cultural elements found their way into the rite of Christian baptism. Unlike in the preceding centuries, the process of baptismal inculturation in this period was characterized by a broader cultural base. The church began to admit into the liturgy of baptism not only suitable initiatory rites from the pagan mystery rites, but also socio-cultural rites that were not strictly connected with idol worship. Its "liturgists" then did this at random, with no overall planning, and with enviable creative spirit. They had, one might say, the fantasy and vigor of youth. Many of the things they did would quite simply be unthinkable today. Yet we cannot reproach them for lacking a sense of responsibility. Though they were not answerable to a central church government, as liturgists are today, they took time to explain to the people the meaning of what the church was doing. What were some of these cultural elements and how were they explained?

Baptismal Anointing

The first time we come across the practice in the western church of anointing the neophytes is in Tertullian's book *On Baptism* which he wrote toward the year 200.[10] We note in passing that also for the first time we receive information regarding the epiclestic blessing of the baptismal water, the mention of the church in the formula of baptism, and the preference for the solemnities of Easter and Pentecost as days for conferring baptism.

As regards anointing, Tertullian records that after baptism the neophytes are anointed, it would seem, on the crown of the head, "as Moses anointed Aaron unto priesthood."[11] He describes the rite as a generous pouring of oil, so unlike the practice prevalent in our time which is mere token. "The oil," he writes, "flows down our bodies." Tertullian explains the meaning of anointing in the context of the anointing performed by Moses on Aaron, namely unto priesthood. Perhaps he was thinking of this when he wrote in his *Exhortation to Chastity*, "are we of the laity not also priests?"[12]

A point of interest here is the origin of this rite. Baptismal anointing is nowhere to be found in the New Testament. In fact, it is not mentioned even by patristic literature prior to Tertullian.[13] We know that certain mystery rites observed the practice, and so it is possible that Christians borrowed it from them. But what makes the practice Christian is the meaning that was attached to it: the priesthood of the baptized. To bring this out, Tertullian employs a biblical type, the anointing of Aaron. Later authors, like Ambrose of Milan and Cyril of Jerusalem, explained the meaning of this postbaptismal anointing in the same way as Tertullian. For instance, Ambrose in his work *The Mysteries* tells the neophytes: "You were anointed that you may become a chosen race, priestly, precious; for we are all anointed unto the kingdom of God and unto priesthood with spiritual grace."[14]

Biblical typology, both from the Old and the New Testaments, was a favorite method among the Fathers for reorienting cultural elements to the Christian mystery. Tertullian applies this method also to the baptismal water, when in connection with it he recalls the water of creation, the great deluge, the Red Sea, and the Jordan river. Biblical typology was probably the best method at hand to insert culture into the stream of salvation history and thus make it a bearer of the Christian mystery.

Besides the postbaptismal anointing there existed another anointing, one given before the baptismal bath. The third-century author of *Apostolic Tradition* distinguishes two kinds of baptismal oil blessed by the bishop: one he calls "oil of thanksgiving" which we today call chrism, the other, "oil of exorcism" or the oil of catechumens. After the rite of renunciation the author directs the presbyter to anoint the candidate with the oil of exorcism, as he prays, "Let all [evil] spirits depart from you." He gives no further explanation of this rite, although the formula clearly points to exorcism.[15] A century later Ambrose of Milan in his mystagogical catechesis *The Sacraments* delivers the following instruction to neophytes regarding the prebaptismal anointing: "You were anointed as an athlete of Christ, as one who will fight the battle of this world."[16] It is difficult to miss the allusion to 1 Corinthians 9:24-27, which describes Christian life in the context of athletes in the arena, though it is unlikely that the rite was introduced with this biblical passage in mind. Yet does not this allusion to athletes allow us to detect the entry of a secular ritual into the rite of Christian baptism? Is it not possible that anointing, whether it was done before or after the sacramental bath, was in some way influenced by the practice of anointing, that is, massaging the body of athletes with oil before the combat?

This could sound trite and banal. However, in the context of early cultures where there was no neat distinction between the sacred and the profane, where the daily preoccupations of life intertwined with the supranatural reality, where mortal combats in the arena were invested with divine purpose, could the "anointing" of athletes be considered trite and banal? And in a situation where neophyte Christians found themselves surrounded by the lures of paganism or were subjected to hostility and persecution, what could have been more meaningful for them than anointing?[17]

Toward the West and the East

Some oriental versions of *Apostolic Tradition*, namely the Sahidic, Arabic, and Ethiopic, direct those who are being baptized to face the west as they renounce Satan. The symbolism is rather obvious. The west is the region where the sun sets, where there is darkness, and hence where Satan ruled. This ritual detail was observed by some churches as far as Milan in the time of Ambrose, but not by the Roman Church which probably did not consider it appropriate.[18] After the rite of renunciation the catechumens faced the east, saying: "Father, Son, and Holy Spirit, I believe in you, I bow before you and place myself at your service."[19] Again the symbolism is obvious. For the early Christians Christ was the *Sol salutis,* and they believed that as Christ had ascended toward the east, he would return on the last day also from the east. Yet we should not disregard the influence of the cult of the sun which was introduced by Emperor Aurelian when he made the *Sol Invictus* the god of the Roman empire. At any rate, the practice of facing the east at the baptismal rite would have received a friendly welcome from the new converts, especially along the Mediterranean where the sun cult was firmly established. As far down as the seventh century the Church of Rome still observed the tradition of facing the east at some parts of the Mass like the *Gloria* and the collect.

Cup of Milk and Honey

A charming baptismal rite, which did not survive the test of time, is referred to in *Apostolic Tradition*. It mentions a cup of milk mixed with honey offered to neophytes between the reception of the consecrated bread and that of the consecrated wine.[20] The positioning of this rite leaves a sharp impression of recklessness. There was doctrinally much at stake as far as the possible popular interpretation of the cup was concerned. But the author takes the necessary precautions. He urges the bishop to explain diligently to the neophytes the meaning of the cup.[21] According to him, the mixed drink symbolizes the "fulfillment of God's promise to our ancestors that he would lead them to a land flowing with milk and honey." The symbol fits perfectly the meaning of baptism as *pascha* or the passage of God's people to the church through the sacramental water of baptism. Having crossed the new Jordan, they enter the new promised land flowing with the eucharistic milk and honey. Ritually the place of the mixed cup in the order of communion seems to strengthen the meaning of the eucharist as the fulfillment of God's promise.

One might be tempted to conclude that since the author uses biblical typology to explain the mixed drink, he must have derived the practice directly from the Old Testament. But this would seem unlikely. Outside the core of apostolic tradition liturgical forms, especially the explanatory rites, seem to have developed not by the process of incorporating biblical elements into the liturgy, but by admitting into it suitable elements of contemporary culture and investing them with biblical meaning. It would be rather amusing to picture the early liturgists reading through the pages of Scripture in search of ritual elements that they could possibly make use of as some sort of introductory or explanatory rites of the liturgy. They were pastors and catechists who had a keen perception of how their people lived their lives in the cultural milieu of the time. They were profoundly cognizant of their people's rituals, needs, and aspirations. These they introduced into the liturgy, so that people could worship with their feet on the ground, so that the liturgy would not be divorced from the reality of human life. They were great liturgists, because they were pastors.

Tertullian alludes to the same practice of offering to the neophytes the cup of milk and honey. In his work, *The Crown*, he writes: "After we have been welcomed [by the bishop], we taste the cup of milk and honey which signifies concord."[22] The word "welcome" roughly translates the Latin *susceptio* or *munus susceptionis* which was the Roman legal term for the father's official claim that the newborn infant was his.[23]

Can we trace the source for the cup of milk and honey in the Roman cultural milieu? The ancient Romans had the custom of giving milk mixed with honey to newborn infants. The drink was expected to strengthen them against sickness and the influence of evil spirits. It was considered to possess an apotropaic quality. But together with the *susceptio* it could also have signified the act of welcoming the infant to the family. Tertullian probably had this in mind when he described the mixed cup as *lactis et mellis concordiam*. But the early church might possibly have been inspired by 1 Peter 2:2's baptismal discourse: "Like the newborn infants you are, you must crave for pure milk." One difficulty with this is the unlikeliness of direct borrowing from scriptural passages. It is not far-fetched to imagine that the Roman custom had its share in the introduction of the cup into Christian rite of initiation. Nor should we lightly dismiss the possible influence of the Eleusinian mystery rite which included the offering of a cup of honeyed drink to the initiates.

White Garment and Lighted Candle

Ambrose of Milan, Gregory of Nyssa, and Cyril of Jerusalem mention the white garment and the lighted candle given to neophytes. The white garment was explained as a symbol of Christian dignity or of the church's baptismal innocence. In *The Mysteries* Ambrose writes: "You received the white garment as sign that you had put off the covering of sins, and had put on the chaste robes of innocence."[24] Again we can ask where and how the rite originated. It could have been inspired by the *toga candida* of the Roman citizens, hence symbolizing the admission of the neophytes into the "heavenly city." There was also the white *toga virilis* worn by Roman boys at the end of their fourteenth year of age, but its similarity to the baptismal garment is not immediately clear. A more likely source is the initiatory white garment used in the Mithraic mystery rite. On the other hand, the use of candles, which Christians until the fourth century did not have because of association with pagan worship, was introduced into the baptismal rite, most probably to illustrate the meaning of baptism as *photismos* or enlightenment.

Washing of Feet

The washing of the feet of neophytes as they ascend from the baptismal pool is attested by Ambrose of Milan in his *The Sacraments*.[25] Ambrose defends this Milanese practice against Roman critics who felt that it was too secular an act to be incorporated into the sacred celebration of baptism. He notes that the Church of Rome itself used to observe it in the past, but "perhaps on account of the multitude [of neophytes] the practice declined." Considering the famous Roman sense for practicality, Ambrose's guess might not be far from the truth. Even today the rite of baptism for children permits the omission of the anointing with chrism if many children are baptized.[26] Ambrose concludes the debate with these lapidary words: "In all things I desire to follow the Church in Rome, yet we too have our common sense. Others elsewhere have the right to keep their practices; we also have as much right to keep ours."

In defense of his local church's practice, Ambrose searched for a biblical basis which he quite easily found in John 13's Last Supper washing of feet. But was this also its direct inspiration and source, or did it serve merely as biblical type? For one thing, this New Testament type is not convincing, especially since it was inserted in the context of a meal, not baptism. But it was his way of giving scriptural force to a local tradition. We may note in passing that Chapter 53 of the sixth-century *Rule of Benedict* directs the abbot and the entire community to wash the feet of guests who come to the monastery. At a time when most people travelled on foot, nothing could have been more soothing than water for one's tired and dusty feet. Washing the feet of guests was a sign of welcome and hospitality. Could this have been the original meaning of this Milanese baptismal rite? It would seem that the washing of feet upon coming up from a pool of water has little sense outside this cultural setting.

Baptismal Terminology

The influence of the pagan mystery rites upon Christian baptism was not confined to ritual gestures. *Photismos* or enlightenment, *loutron* or bath, *mystagogia* or the initiatory instruction, *mystes* or the instructor, and *myomenos* or the initiate were words the pagans shared with Christians. These were words whose meaning an average Christian would have easily grasped and probably used with a certain awareness that pagans had entered them even earlier in their religious lexicon.

But the influence did not come only from mystery rites. In the writings of Tertullian dealing with baptism we come across words that possessed a legal character. Tertullian, it will be remembered, was a jurist. In his book, *The Crown*, he calls the rite of baptismal renunciation *eiuratio*. This legal term was used to indicate cessation of contractual service. Applied to baptism, it implies that the Christian has disclaimed all further obligation to serve the devil. In another book, *The Spectacles*, Tertullian speaks of the baptismal profession of faith as *sacramenti testatio* and *signaculum fidei*.[27] These terms likewise had a legal force. They were used in reference to the oath of allegiance soldiers swore to the emperor. Used for baptism, they reminded the Christians that they had solemnly vowed to serve Christ alone and with absolute loyalty. By employing such legal terms Tertullian impressed a certain juridical character on the neophytes' act of renunciation and profession of faith. He seems to tell them that these were serious things that should not be taken lightly.

* * * * * * * *

From this historical review of the rite of baptism in the early church we gather the following information.

1. The core of the New Testament tradition on baptism, which consists of washing in water with the trinitarian formula, was the axis around which the ritual shape of baptism in the early church developed. It is not easy to determine the role culture played in the ritual elaboration of the baptismal bath and the wording of the formula. From an early period immersion seems to have been the normal way of washing, though infusion must, on occasion, have also been admitted. Likewise, preference was expressed for running or living water, probably to stress symbolism. At least by the third century the baptismal water was already being blessed in an epiclestic manner and explained in the light of biblical typology. The formula itself, as early as the second century, seems to have been already elaborated in a credal form. In the third century it developed fully into the form of the creed and would stay so until the ninth century, when the short declarative form was introduced in the western church.

2. The pagan mystery rites have imprinted unmistakable marks on Christian baptism. Both the ritual and verbal elements of these rites found their way into the baptismal celebration. Several words like *mystagogia* and *mystes* have become part of standard Christian vocabulary. On the other hand, some symbols that could have been derived from mystery rites, like the giving of white garment and the lighted candle, are now part of the baptismal practice in the Roman Church. The church's program of incorporating pagan initiatory rites, provided these did not obscure Christian faith, can be explained by the nature of baptism as a rite of initiation. This tradition of openness to non-Christian rites of initiation, provided they are compatible with the Christian rite, was revived by Vatican II's Constitution on Liturgy (art. 65).

3. Other cultural elements, which did not necessarily belong to the body of the mystery rites, also exerted influence on the baptismal liturgy. Examples are prebaptismal anointing, washing of feet, the cup of milk and honey, and the legal terms used by Tertullian when he spoke of baptismal renunciation and commitment. It seems that at a certain point in history the moral implication of baptism, such as absolute loyalty to Christ and the Church's faith, especially in times of persecution, led Tertullian to adopt legal terms that would bring home the moral aspect of baptism.

4. Underlying all this was an attempt to bring the Christian liturgy closer to the experience of people. Concretely this meant admitting into the baptismal liturgy those suitable elements from religious and other cultural traditions that were able to illustrate the meaning of the sacrament. In several instances these elements became part of the introductory or the explanatory rites of the baptismal liturgy. Thus while the apostolic core of baptism remained basically the washing in water with the trinitarian formula, new elements were introduced to elaborate the ritual shape of baptism. This process is what is known today as inculturation. It aims ultimately to render the baptismal rite culturally accessible to people, because it is expressed in words, actions, and symbols with which they are familiar.

5. The early church used a method that is called biblical typology. After considering whether a particular religious or cultural element was suitable for the baptismal liturgy, the early liturgists searched in Sacred Scriptures for a corresponding or appropriate type. This was part of the process of critiquing culture, of being countercultural. The idea was to reorient the meaning of the cultural element, so that it could enrich the people's understanding of the sacrament. It was a matter of reinterpreting culture in the light or context of the Christian mystery. Sometimes the biblical types have only a vague or distant similarity with the cultural element, or they might even ignore its original meaning. This was part of being countercultural. From the cultural standpoint, anthropologists might regard this as a negative aspect of biblical typology. The mixed cup of milk and honey, for example, fits the paschal dimension of baptism, but its original cultural meaning is not at all evoked by the Exodus typology. In other words, we should also consider the question of cultural evocation when we introduce cultural elements into the liturgy. James 5:14, which deals with the anointing of the sick, is a fine example of cultural evocation: oil was normally used to soothe the pain of the sick. Nonetheless, biblical typology has the distinction of allowing culture to participate in salvation history as it unfolds in sacramental celebrations.

6. In conclusion, we may note with envy and admiration how the early liturgists were filled with creative and venturesome spirit. This was, of course, possible, because they were not

directly responsible to a central government. For example, the cup of milk and honey offered to neophytes at their first communion was surely at the fringes of what was acceptable because of the real risk of misinterpretation. Today such a practice would simply be unthinkable. But alas times have changed. Yet something of the youthful boldness and creativity of the early liturgists is always needed by the church. And this is what inculturation is able to bring about within the confines of what liturgical tradition allows.

Notes

1. *Didaché*, ed. W. Rordorf and A. Tuilier, Sources chrétiennes, vol. 248 (1978) 7, pp. 170-71. W. Rordorf, "Le baptême selon la Didaché," in *Mélanges liturgiques offerts à Dom Botte* (Louvain, 1972) 499-510.

2. *La Tradition Apostolique de Saint Hippolyte*, ed. B. Botte (Münster, 1989) no. 21, pp. 48-50. M. Metzger: "Enquêtes autour de la prétendue Tradition Apostolique," *Ecclesia Orans* 9:1 (1992) 7-36.

3. *Didaché* 7, p. 172. Prebaptismal fasting is clearly distinguished from the ascetical fasting enjoined on Christians every Wednesday and Friday by the author.

4. Possibly the first six chapters of the *Didaché* on the two ways are what chapter 7 refers to: "After the foregoing instructions, baptize ..." See note 3 of the editors.

5. Ed. L. Pautigny (Paris, 1904); partial English translation by W. Jurgens, *The Faith of the Early Fathers* (Collegeville, 1970) 50-56.

6. *First Apology* 61; Jurgens 54.

7. E. Yarnold, "Baptism and the Pagan Mysteries in the Fourth Century," *The Heythrop Journal* 13 (1972) 247-267.

8. *First Apology* 61; Jurgens 54.

9. According to E. Yarnold, "apart from common terminology, there are other striking points of resemblance between the Christian and pagan ceremonies themselves: scrutinies, catechesis, the learning of sacred formulas, fasting, stripping, anointing, immersion, the putting on of a white robe, consignation (even with a permanently visible sign in the form of a tattoo or brand), a meal of initiation (a honeyed drink forms part of both the Eleusinian rites and the neophyte's first communion) all feature in both Christian and pagan rites." Ibid. 135.

10. *De Baptismo*, Corpus Christianorum, vol. 1:1 (1954) 277-295. B. Botte, "Le symbolisme de l'huile et de l'onction," *Questions liturgiques* 62 (1981) 196-208.

11. *De Baptismo* 7, p. 282.

12. *De Exhortatione Castitatis*, Corpus Christianorum, vol. 1:1 (1954) 7, p. 1024.

13. B. Botte thinks that the following statement of Tertullian in *De Corona* (chapter 3) refers to baptismal anointing: *Hanc si nulla scriptura determinavit, certa consuetudo corroboravit, quae sine dubio de traditione manavit.* The text seems, however, to refer to *linea serra*.

14. *De Sacramentis/De Mysteriis*, ed. B. Botte, Sources chrétiennes, vol. 25bis (1961) 6, p. 117.

15. La Tradition Apostolique de Saint Hippolyte, no. 21, p. 46. R. Cabié, "L'initiation chez Hippolyte," in *Mens Concordet Voci* (Paris, 1983) 544-558.

16. *De Sacramentis* 1,4, p. 55.

17. G. Winkler, "The Original Meaning of the Prebaptismal Anointing and its Implications," *Worship* 52 (1978) 24-25.

18. *De Mysteriis* 2, p. 109.

19. *La Tradition Apostolique*, note, p. 46.

20. *Lac et melle mixta simul ad plenitudinem promissionis quae ad patres fuit, quam dixit terram fluentem lac et mel.* 21, p. 56.

21. *De universis vero his rationem reddat episcopus eis qui percipiunt.* Ibid.

22. *De Corona*, Corpus Christianorum, vol. 2:2 (1954) 1042-1043: Inde suscepti lactis et mellis concordiam praegustamus. Note the temporal relationship between *suscepti* and *praegustamus*.

23. *Susceptio* in this legal context is echoed by the *Rule of St. Benedict*, c. 58 which carries the title *De DisciplinaSuscipiendorum Fratrum* (Collegeville, 1981) 266.

24. *De Mysteriis* 7, p. 118.

25. *De Sacramentis* III,1, pp. 72-74.

26. *Ordo Baptismi Parvulorum*, ed. typica altera (Vatican City, 1986), no. 24, p. 20.

27. *De Spectaculis*, Corpus Christianorum, vol. 1:1 (1954) 24, p. 248.

2

The Cultural and Domestic Tradition of the Eucharist

BY TRADITION THE EUCHARIST HAS BEEN REGARDED AND CELEBRATED AS A meal, even if at times it is hardly recognizable as such. Thin wafers and communion from the cup by the presider alone dispossess it of, or at least weaken, its meal symbolism. Likewise several key words that pertain to it, like sanctuary, altar, and priest, are strikingly sacrificial in tone. We have grown used to expressions like "sacrifice of the Mass" (Mass here means the sacrament), "unbloody sacrifice" (the meal of bread and wine is unbloody sacrifice), and "sacrificial banquet" (the sacrificial character is somewhat softened here). These are attempts to balance the two poles. The actual *ordo* of the celebration makes the same attempt. The eucharist is both meal and sacrifice, but what does its *ordo*, that is, the composite of texts and symbolic elements, look like?[1]

The confusion between the theological content of the eucharist, which is the paschal sacrifice of Christ, and its liturgical shape, which is his supper, is at the root of the long-standing controversy between Roman Catholics and Lutherans.[2] In reality, however, both sides detect in the eucharistic liturgy something of meal and sacrifice, with particular stress on one or the other. Today more and more Roman Catholics call the Mass the Lord's Supper and speak of the eucharistic altar as table and of the priest as presider. On the other hand, Lutherans continue to call the eucharistic table altar. Though the content and form of the

19

eucharist can and should be neatly distinguished, if we want to do theology, they are inseparable, and they tend to intrude into each other. This is why the eucharistic liturgy cannot be reduced to a mere fellowship meal nor to a purely sacrificial action. Whereas its liturgical shape should clearly express its meal aspect, it should not ignore its fundamental meaning: it is an *anamnesis* and hence the real presence of Christ's unrepeatable sacrifice. The statement "the Mass is Christ's sacrifice," which is a theological shortcut of "the Mass is the sacrament [meal form] of Christ's sacrifice," has immensely contributed to the confusion between content and form.[3]

But it seems that a more useful approach to the question is to view the eucharistic liturgy as a domestic celebration. There is much to be said in favor of G. Dix's assertion that "the apostolic and primitive church regarded all christian worship, and especially the eucharist, as a highly *private* activity, and rigidly excluded all strangers from taking any part in it whatsoever, and even from attendance at the eucharist. Christian worship was intensely corporate, but it was not public." He goes on to say that by origin and by nature the eucharist was not meant to be a "public" affair in the sense that we have come to accept, like a concert on Sunday in the park, "but a highly *exclusive* thing, whose original setting is entirely domestic and private.[4] The domestic character of the eucharist is very much at the core of its later development as a liturgical action. Indeed the place of celebration, language, vessels, and music revolved originally around this domestic nucleus. Whereas theological thinking, and subsequently liturgical practice, sometimes heavily underlined the sacrificial aspect of the eucharist, to the extent of regarding the place of celebration as temple, the dining table as altar, and the presider as priest, its domestic character has never been totally ignored.

The stress on the domestic character of the eucharist might be criticized as being countercultural. In many parts of the world, modern life moves with frightful velocity and families seldom enjoy the leisure of a meal at home. Among some pastors there is even a lurking temptation to be relevant to this contemporary situation by patterning the eucharistic celebration after the style of fast-food counters, or by reducing it to some form of meal service imitating the salient features of fast-foods which have made them so popular today, namely, open twenty-four hours, unvaried selection of courses, eat and run. If there is anything the eucharist is able to preach to families of our time, perhaps it is the ideal of a home, of a family gathered around the table to share God's blessings and the fruit of human labor. In this sense, the eucharist is indeed countercultural: it serves as a leaven of family unity in a world broken by individualism. As G. Dix has pointed out, "even in a nominally christian world, the eucharist has always retained some of the characteristics of a private domestic gathering of the 'household of God'."[5] Sometimes one wonders at the message that is projected by eucharistic celebrations in open air or in a football stadium, in the anonymity of a huge assembly. Is the eucharist on such occasions perceived as the supper of God's household, or is it perhaps used as a triumphant manifestation of Catholic faith?

This chapter focuses on a number of elements of the eucharistic liturgy that show how the early church developed the shape of the celebration in the cultural setting and context of a home. Of particular interest are such components of the celebration as the place, language, rites, and vessels. These are examined in the light of the domestic character of the eucharist. The question of music is treated in Chapter 4.

PLACE FOR CELEBRATION

The Acts of the Apostles (2:46) depicts an idealized portrait of the Christian community which gathered "day by day attending the temple together and breaking bread in their homes, partaking of food with glad and generous hearts". Acts 20:7-12 records the Sunday breaking of bread presided over by Paul "in the upper chamber" of a house in Troas. The eucharist, the specific and characteristic celebration of Christians, was held at home. It is evident that from the earliest times the eucharist was regarded as a domestic liturgy. The disciples of Jesus attended the temple and synagogue services, but they did not, or more precisely could not, break bread in those places. For neither the temple nor the synagogue was ever meant to be a place for a fellowship meal. The temple was for sacrifices and the synagogue for the proclamation of the word and community prayers. Fellowship meals, like the eucharist, were held at home.

This was the tradition the church brought with it when it moved out of Palestine. Before the year 165 Justin Martyr wrote that the Christians of Rome, "whether they live in the city or the countryside, gather together in one place" to celebrate the eucharist.[6] Justin prudently does not specify the "place," for in time of persecution this would be revealing to the Roman emperor the place where Christians gathered. Of course, there is no reason to believe that the place was not the home of one of them. In the year 304 the reader Emeritus bravely admitted to the proconsul of Carthage that "it is in my house that we hold the *dominicum*," that is, the Lord's meal.[7] Converts offered the use of their homes which, in the Roman tradition, were usually a four-sided structure built around an open courtyard with a well of water at the center. The *triclinium* or dining room, especially if the house belonged to a wealthy family, could easily be rearranged for the celebration of the eucharist.[8] Rome claims several such houses which can still be visited under the churches of John and Paul, Cecilia, Clement, and Pudentiana. But such houses, even if they were large, might not easily accommodate large assemblies. As the community grew in number, a larger space was needed for the assembly.

Since persecutions were sporadic occurrences, in time of peace Christians acquired ordinary houses and adapted them permanently to the requirements of the liturgy. The story is told of Emperor Alexander Severus (+235) who preferred to sell to Christians a house that was in the public domain, "for it would be better that a god, of whatever sort, be adored there rather than to use the building for the sale of drinks."[9] The houses owned or bought by the Christian community for their worship came to be known as *domus ecclesiae*, the house of the community. In the course of time this name was shortened to *ecclesia*, the church building. From here is derived the theology of the house church as the image of the church community. A famous example of such houses of the church was the third-century house at Dura-Europos on the Euphrates. It had a function room of around 16 feet by 43 feet, which served for the eucharistic assembly, and a smaller room probably for baptistery, as the fresco of Christ walking on the water suggests.[10]

After the conversion of Emperor Constantine there came a dramatic shift from the simplicity of homes to the splendor of imperial basilicas. The domestic dining room gave way to the large public halls where formerly the emperor, seated on the throne, had held court and given audiences. Yet for all its imposing majesty, what was the basilica but basically one of the function rooms of a Roman house? There was, of course, more space: a larger nave for the assembly and ample room in the sanctuary for the table, ambo, presidential chair, and seats for the presbyters and ministers. The long and short of it is that even in the basilica the eucharist retained the essential traits of a domestic liturgy, though on a larger scale. When Constantine decreed in the year 321 the observance of Sunday rest in the empire, the celebration of the eucharist acquired a more solemn character. Surely the atmosphere and ambience of the imperial hall would, at any rate, have demanded a corresponding liturgical splendor. Prayer formularies took on a more solemn, hieratic, and rhetorical form; gestures imitated the imperial court ceremonials; and the music became more elaborate requiring trained performers.[11]

The first Christian basilica was the Lateran palace, *palatium imperii nostri lateranense*, which Constantine gave as a gift to Pope Sylvester. The emperor ordered the construction of new basilicas for Christian use: on the Vatican hill where the Apostle Peter was buried, at Via Ostiense where the Apostle Paul suffered martyrdom, at Campo Verano where the deacon Lawrence was buried, and in several other places in Italy. His mother Helena, on her part, had the basilicas in Bethlehem, Nazareth, and Jerusalem built to commemorate the events of Christ's life. These roofed structures were rectangular in shape and divided into three or five naves marked by rows of columns. At the far end of the apse was the *cathedra* or chair of the bishop, surrounded by benches for the presbyters and ministers.[12]

Architecture, which is one of the finer expressions of a people's culture, has immensely influenced the development of the shape of the eucharist from the intimacy of a home gathering to an awesome imperial convocation. The influence of the basilica, as we shall have occasion to see, was felt in both the rites and the language of the celebration. Through the centuries the architectural and artistic design of the *domus ecclesiae* has continued to undergo remarkable modifications from the romanesque to the gothic, from the renaissance to the baroque, from the neoclassic to the modern and postmodern.[13] But beneath such variations one can perceive the original core: the eucharist is a meal which is properly celebrated at home, regardless of how the cultural setting determines the architecture of the house.

The early Christians, whether for theological or practical reasons, chose not to celebrate in temples, whose *cella* would have been too dark and small and whose open colonnades would have been most unsuitable for a meal. Nor did they gather for the eucharist in the tiny, dark underground rooms of the Roman catacombs, which being public burial places would have been the worst place for gathering in time of persecutions, not to mention the prospect of celebrating the Lord's Supper amidst entombed bodies. The early church celebrated at home or in one of their homes or in a house the community had acquired. For the eucharist is a meal: it is the supper of the Lord. Attempts to pattern new churches after the temples of other religions, like pagodas and mosques, miss altogether the point about the Lord's supper as a domestic liturgy. They also miss the point which R. Cabié in his *The Eucharist* has expressed with profound insight. The house of the church, rather than the temple, signifies the welcome and hospitality the eucharistic community shows to strangers and the poor with whom it shares the same faith in Christ. It "challenges the divisions that run through human society." Cabié presses the point to its limits, when he writes: "a special welcome is to be given to the poor, even if the bishop has to surrender his chair and sit on the floor."[14]

Origen fittingly sums up what we have discussed so far regarding the domestic ambient of the eucharist. In his *Homily on Jeremiah* he writes: "Those who celebrate the pasch as Jesus wants will not stay on the lower floor of the house; rather those who celebrate the feast with Jesus go up to the great hall, to the lighted hall, to the adorned hall which is prepared for the feast. If you go up with him to celebrate the pasch, he gives you the cup of the new covenant; he also gives you the bread of blessing: he gives you the gift of his own body and blood."[15] Though the text, coming as it does from Origen, is allegorical, it allows us to catch a glimpse of how the church in the third century readied the "upper chamber" of their house for the celebration of the eucharist. The "upper chamber," he explains, signifies hospitality, which the widow showed to Elisha when she readied for the man of God the upper room of her house (2 Kgs 4:10). The feast to which Jesus invites us is held in the great hall on the upper floor; it is lighted and adorned, as befits the Lord's supper. The domestic quality of the eucharist does not subtract from its festive character. It does not lead to banality and improvisation. Domesticity, to rephrase a proverb, does not breed contempt.

THE INFLUENCE OF LATIN ON
EUCHARISTIC FORMULARIES

An element of the eucharistic celebration, and of the liturgy as a whole, that has been strongly conditioned by culture is the corpus of the early liturgical formularies. The use of living or current language in public worship necessarily involves inculturation in the deepest sense of the word. Language is not merely a compendium of words and phrases; it is above all the mirror of a people's pattern of thought and values. It expresses, in other words, their cultural trait and identity.[16] This is why, the option of the early church in the west to use Greek and Latin, that is, the living languages of its converts, opened the door wide to inculturation. What this means is that the church formulated the Gospel it preached using the cultural patterns, indeed the philosophical system of thought, of the Greeks and the Romans. For the liturgy this meant that Greek and Latin became its languages. But this was not all. Greek and Latin were not merely vehicles of communication. Because languages contain and mirror the culture of the people, Greek and Latin impressed on liturgical formularies the thought and value patterns of Greeks and Romans. Thus we may say that the liturgy not only spoke Greek and Latin; in effect it became Greek and Latin.

To appreciate the role of language in the development of liturgical texts, it might be helpful to recall briefly the history of the liturgical language in the first four centuries.[17]

Outside Palestine and Syria, Greek *koiné* was the *lingua franca* of most people in both the eastern and the western regions of the Roman empire. *Koiné* differed from classical and literary Greek in that *koiné* was of a popular type. By the year 40 and certainly 64, when the church in Rome was established, the prevalent language in the City was *koiné*. It had become the language of the empire, and the Roman citizens themselves spoke it. It is interesting to note that during the first two centuries, ten out of the fourteen bishops of Rome were Greek-speaking. It was to be expected that the Roman Church would use the *koiné* in the liturgy and official documents.

The process of the latinization of the liturgy began, not in Rome, but in Northern Africa, thanks to the efforts of Tertullian, Cyprian, Arnobius, Lactantius, and Augustine. From these writers we inherited the use in the liturgy of words like *plebs* or assembly, *sacramentum, ordo,* and *institutio.* These words did not originate in a religious milieu, but by force of usage they acquired a distinct liturgical meaning. When Tertullian, for instance, spoke of the baptismal promises as *sacramenti testatio,* he was imposing a Christian meaning on a legal phrase.[18] From Northern Africa these and similar words found their way into the eucharistic formularies of the Roman Church. Likewise, the first authorized Latin translation of Scripture for use in the eucharist appeared, not in Rome, but in Africa around the year 250.

The first attempt to introduce Latin into the liturgy of Rome came from Pope Victor I, an African by birth, who died in 203. His success was partial. The language of the Roman liturgy, until the fourth century, remained in a state of transition. It was bilingual, although by the third century Rome was speaking Latin again. It was never an easy matter for the Roman Church to abandon its traditions. Compromise was a preferred solution. Thus the prayer formularies continued to be in Greek, but the scriptural readings were now in Latin. Not until the papacy of Damasus I, who died in 384, did a definitive transition from Greek to Latin take place in the eucharistic celebration of the City. It happened a century too late, but it was nonetheless a courageous enterprise for a church known for venerating its traditions. We should not regard this as being romantic, but is it not rather difficult to abandon the language used in apostolic times and the age of martyrs in favor of the current language? The next time around, it took several hundred years for the Roman Church to come to the realization that outside and even inside the Vatican walls people spoke in languages other than Latin.

From the fourth to the late sixth century the Roman Church developed the Latin liturgical language.[19] Even the Roman liturgy was not built in one day. Those were centuries of an intense creativity that produced several classic prayers for eucharistic use, like collects, prayers over the gifts, prayers after communion, and prayers over the assembly. These texts have come down to us in sacramentaries or, as these books came to be known from the Middle Ages, missals. A good number of these compositions are preserved in the Roman Missal of Paul VI. The chief authors of the early Roman texts were none other than the bishops of Rome: Damasus, Innocent I, Leo the Great, Gelasius, Vigilius, and Gregory the Great. The literary style of the formularies indicates that their authors received their education from the Roman schools of rhetoric, arts, and classical studies. The long and short of it is that the style of their composition and the product itself pertained more to the segment of the Roman elite than to the ordinary people.

It would be too unkindly to deal here in detail with the different literary forms employed by the authors of the Latin formularies. For the sake of completeness, however, it might be useful to mention typical examples, like binary succession, antithesis, *cursus*, and *concinnitas* or symmetry.[20] One of the remarkable rhetorical traits of the early Latin formularies is the *cursus*, which was perfected by Pope Leo the Great.[21] It consists of the rhythmic arrangement of the last word of a line for the sake of cadence and sometimes also to suggest such sentiments as joy and wonder. The vowel length and the accents, both principal and secondary, given to such words constitute what are known to specialists as the *cursus planus, tardus*, and *velox*. By their arrangement and composition they are able to produce the desired cadence and sentiments. This is a type of rhetorical device that must have immensely pleased the listeners, provided they belonged to the class of the elites.

A classic example is the Christmas collect composed by Leo the Great, found in the Sacramentary of Verona: *Deus, qui humanae substantiae dignitatem et mirabiliter condidisti et mirabilius reformasti . . ."*[22] The verbs *condidisti* and *reformasti* are both in the *cursus velox*, and they express the sentiments of admiration, joy, and gratitude for God's work of creation and salvation in Christ. One quality of the *cursus* is its ability to imply such sentiments in the way the words are arranged, without the need to employ explicitly the verbs and substantives of admiration, joy, and gratitude. It is not necessary to say "we admire and thank you for creating humankind"; the *cursus* takes care of that. It is possible to imagine that on any cold Christmas night a good number of the assembly would not have caught the theology behind Pope Leo's dense formulary, but they would have delighted to listen to its rhythmic cadences, symmetrical arrangement of phrases, antithetical construction, and play of words.

Besides the rhetorical quality of Latin, there was another cultural factor that influenced the early eucharistic texts. It is the proverbial Roman sobriety, which the great scholar E. Bishop has called "the genius of the Roman rite."[23] There is agreement among historians today that what used to be regarded as the "sensuousness" of the Roman liturgy was actually not of Roman origin but of Franco-Germanic making. Sensuousness in this sense referred to those medieval symbols and formularies which stirred religious sentiments or encouraged some undefinable experience of awe and wonder in the presence of God's mystery. The Romans were a sober and practical people whose language was equally sober and direct. Thus the Roman prayers for the eucharist that date around the fifth century avoid colorful and picturesque words or words tending to arouse human emotions.

A cursory examination of the collects in the early sacramentaries reveals a language addressed to the intellect rather than to the heart of the listeners. Today only a few would probably link the following collect of the Gregorian Sacramentary to the Christmas feast: *Deus, qui hanc sacratissimam noctem veri luminis fecisti inlustratione clarescere; da, quaesumus, ut cuius lucis mysteria in terra cognovimus, eius quoque gaudiis in caelo perfruamur.*[24] Translated literally, the text reads: "God, you made this most holy night resplendent with the clarity of the true light. Grant, we pray, that we may experience in heaven the joy of him, whose mystery of light we have come to know on earth." This text, composed for the winter solstice or victory of light over the darkness of winter, understandably focuses on the element of light. But it requires special catechesis to show the association of the feast of Christmas to the winter solstice.

Roman sobriety is even more striking in the prayers after communion. Whereas medieval prayers often spoke of the sacramental bread and wine quite simply and directly as the body and blood of Christ, the Roman prayers, in keeping with the *romana sobrietas*, rarely mentioned them. Rather they tend to confine their language to such expressions as "sacraments," "heavenly bread," "food and drink," and "heavenly gifts." Not that the early church in Rome did not believe in the real presence, but it was not part of the church's cultural pattern to depict the mystery with vivid imagery. We have grown used to being told at communion "the body of Christ" and "the blood of Christ." But the Romans of the classical period would have been rather uncomfortable hearing these words at communion time as they received the consecrated bread in their hand.

The Roman Canon, which is quoted in part by Ambrose of Milan, is thoroughly imbued with the culture of classical Rome. Its language portrays the Roman taste for a certain gravity in speech as well as simultaneous redundance and brevity. Such phrases as *te igitur, hanc igitur,* and *unde et memores,* at the start of a sentence are elegant, hieratic, and solemn. They are difficult to capture in translation. The use of the title *Clementissime Pater* gives the Roman Canon an imperial tone, and so does the phrase *supplices te rogamus ac petimus.* True to its sacrificial orientation, the Roman Canon uses pre-Christian sacrificial expressions like *accepta habeas.* It has incorporated also a pagan funeral inscription, namely *refrigerium lucis et pacis.* The legalistic Roman mentality resonates in the threefold declarations *haec dona, haec munera, haec sancta sacrificia inlibata* and *hostiam puram, hostiam sanctam, hostiam immaculatam.* Lastly, the Roman Canon observes balance in its structure. Balance, which is akin to equanimity, was highly prized by the Romans. This is especially evident in the mementoes of the living and the dead and the double commemoration of saints before and after the narration of the Last Supper.[25]

This rather brief review of the Latin liturgical language reveals how Roman culture has profoundly influenced the texts for the eucharistic liturgy of the early church. The liturgy was not only in Latin, it was expressed in a highly cultivated Latin, in a kind of *Kulturlatein* demanded by the solemn ambit of the Roman basilica but not necessarily by the familiar setting of a home. Thus, it was accessible almost exclusively to the educated segment of the Roman Church. The majority spoke the *Volkslatein.* In this sense the language of the liturgy itself became rather exclusive: it failed to welcome the masses. It was not congenial for expressing the supreme value of the eucharistic liturgy, namely hospitality to all regardless of a person's station and attainment in life. Today we put stock, and rightly so, on the ministry of hospitality by trained ushers, but do not our liturgical formularies by their "otherness" often exclude a large segment of the assembly? Should not our hospitality engage the assembly in the dialogue that goes on between God and the church? One may, of course, argue in favor of *Kulturlatein*, that after all we set apart for the worship of God what is most noble in culture. We are all the more disposed to favor such an argument, when not infrequently we witness banality in the liturgy. But the difficulty we face today with this venerable corpus of eucharistic texts is how to translate faithfully its content and also equivalently its extraordinary literary style.

INFLUENCE OF THE IMPERIAL COURT CEREMONIAL

Justin Martyr in his *First Apology*, gives us information on the shape of the Sunday eucharist as it was celebrated in the second century, presumably in a Roman house church.[26] The format of the celebration consisted basically of what are known today as liturgy of the word and liturgy of the eucharist. The liturgy of the word began with readings, by a lector, from both the "memoirs of the Apostles" and the "writings of the prophets," that is, from the New and Old Testament books. This was followed by an explanation of the readings or homily by the *proëstós*, the presider, and concluded by prayers of intercession. The kiss of peace was given at this point, at least when baptism preceded the eucharist. The liturgy of the eucharist began with the presentation (we may presume by the assembly) of bread and wine mixed with water, followed by a "long prayer" recited by the presider. At the end of the prayer the assembly answered "Amen." The second part ended with the distribution of the eucharistic bread and wine by deacons. After the celebration, offerings were made for the poor, widows, and transients of the community. As early as the second century the format of the eucharist, which no longer included the *agape* of the apostolic period though it was still a home celebration, was already sufficiently defined to become the type and exemplar of the Roman eucharistic celebration.

The information of Justin, however, gives no clue as to how, if at all, the Greco-Roman culture influenced the celebration of the eucharist. We presume that the language used was the *koiné*, that the bread and wine were those found in the region, and that the place of gathering was the home of one of the converts. Other than these the cultural setting of the eucharist can only be guessed. While the baptismal liturgy had, as early as the second century, already assimilated traits of the pagan mystery rites, the eucharist did not seem to have been affected by the communion rites of pagan initiations. On the contrary, the liturgy of the word appears to have been a direct descendant of the synagogal service, while the liturgy of the eucharist seems to have been patterned after the Last Supper narrative or at least focused on it.

It was after the fourth century that the ritual shape of the eucharist began to be increasingly bound up with the culture of the period, thanks largely to the conversion of Emperor Constantine and the Edict of Milan in the year 313. For Rome and the other metropolitan cities, especially in the east, culture meant, concretely, the culture of the imperial court. Under the patronage of the emperor himself the church quite understandably assimilated into its liturgy some of the ceremonials of the "ruling class." Unfortunately, our chief document, *Roman Ordo I*, dates from the seventh century or the end of the sixth at the earliest, and hence is a rather late record of what transpired between the fourth and the seventh century.[27] However, historical studies supply us with helpful information regarding this time gap.[28] We may reckon that what the *Roman Ordo* describes originated in the time of Constantine or at least during the Constantinian era.

The so-called *Donatio Constantini*, which is quoted by the *Liber Pontificalis*,[29] reports that Constantine gave to Pope Sylvester the Lateran palace as a gift and authorized him to use the imperial insignia, including the throne, and the privilege to have his portrait hung in public halls. We know that in the year 318 Constantine conferred on the bishops, for good or ill—often ill—the power of jurisdiction in civil proceedings. In the process they received titles, insignia, and privileges that belonged to the office of State dignitaries. It was a kind of marriage that produced unwanted offspring. On the other hand, the *Constitutio*

Constantini, forged around the year 750 under Pope Stephen II, tried to establish the legal basis for the papacy's temporal claims against Byzantium. The document concludes with these menacing words: "Whoever shall transgress these provisions which hold good for all time shall burn in hell with the devil and all the ungodly."[30]

The eucharistic liturgy described by *Roman Ordo I* was the solemn papal Mass celebrated at the Basilica of St. Mary Major on the Esquiline hill on Easter Sunday morning before the year 700. It is not possible nor is it necessary to describe here the entire procedure, which was long and quite complicated. Our interest is in several of its elements which are strikingly imperial in character. The historian T. Klauser has identified them for us.[31] The pope rode on horseback from the Lateran palace to the stational basilica. He was accompanied by the mayor and other dignitaries of the city. He wore the *cappa magna*, a cloak that reached to the feet of the horse. This was a garb worn by the emperor for solemn processions. As the pope walked to the sacristy, two deacons supported him ritually on either side. This was a court ceremonial known as *sustentatio*. In the sacristy his ministers surrounded him, as demanded by the Byzantine court ceremonial, in order to assist him as he vested for the liturgy. He put on an insignia called the *pallium* over the chasuble. It is a white woolen band with pendants in front and at the back. This is originally another imperial insignia of authority. Today it is worn by the pope and metropolitan bishops. Although the *Roman Ordo* does not mention the ring, the special shoes, and the *camelaucum*, which later developed into the miter, we may presume that he wore these imperial insignia as well.[32]

As the pope processed to the sanctuary, he was preceded by acolytes bearing seven lighted torches or candles and a censer, while the *schola cantorum* of men and boys sang the introit or entrance song. We note that candles and incense were used in solemn processions to honor the emperor, and that he was greeted by a choir of singers when he entered an assembly hall for public audiences. Before proclaiming the gospel, the deacon genuflected before the pope to kiss his shoes and to receive his blessing. This curious gesture of kissing the feet was required by the Byzantine court ceremonial. Ministers who served the pope waited on him at the throne and the altar with covered hands, again as demanded by imperial ceremonial. He took communion not at the table but at his throne.

Strangely, the splendor of the imperial court was confined mostly to the entrance rite. Thus the liturgy of the word was celebrated with less pomp, and the liturgy of the eucharist with the proverbial *romana sobrietas* which verged on austerity and gravity. During the eucharistic prayer, for instance, the pope stood at the altar alone and recited the prayer with no further ceremonies and without the assistance of hovering and ubiquitous masters of ceremonies. No candles were brought into the sanctuary at the words of consecration, no bells were rung, no incensation of the sacred species was made, and there were no genuflections and signs of the cross. Thus the core or nucleus of the eucharistic liturgy, namely the word and the sacrament, remained practically untouched by the drama and pomp of the imperial court ceremonial.

Another quality of the Roman culture that survived the incursion of the imperial ceremonial was the sense of practicality which was deeply rooted in Roman civilization. The papal Mass regarded the entrance, offertory, and communion songs as songs of accompaniment. This is why, when the activities they accompanied were over, no less than the pope himself signaled to the choir to stop singing. Altar cloths were not spread until the time of the offertory rite, and presumably they were removed after the celebration, as the Roman rite still does after the eucharist of Holy Thursday. The washing of hands at the offertory, which acquired a symbolic meaning during the early Middle Ages, seems to have been dictated by table hygiene.

We gather from this description of the Roman eucharistic celebration before the eighth century that there were two distinct cultural forces at work. One was the ceremonial of the imperial court; the other was the native Roman quality of sobriety and practical sense. Some have expressed reservations about the elite character of the celebration or the political overtones of the insignia used during the liturgy. Surely this type of inculturation need not become a paradigm for the church today. Though the liturgical insignia of bishops no longer suggest political power but only ecclesiastical leadership, one wonders if there are no viable contemporary alternatives. A missionary bishop considered substituting the miter with the plumed headdress worn by tribal chieftains, but alas this form of inculturation does not free the church and the liturgy from the entanglement with the Constantinian court ceremonials. There is more to inculturation than the change brought about by external adaptation. The miter and the plumed headdress send the same signal: church authority patterned after the imperial system rather than the earlier concept of shepherding. And certainly liturgical leadership in word and sacrament for which bishops are ordained should not be turned into a caste system.[33]

This period, however, seems to tell us that when the church in Rome, and the same must be said of Constantinople, decided to inculturate the shape of the eucharist, it chose what was noble, beautiful, and significant in the culture of the people. The period under discussion should not in any way be so idealized as to suggest that churches today assimilate only what is elite and exclusive in their culture. What it suggests is that, regardless of the socio-economic condition of the people, the eucharistic celebration should be noble, dignified, and beautiful. And nobility of spirit, dignity, and beauty are not an exclusive possession of the elite and the powerful.

EARLY EUCHARISTIC FURNISHINGS

By tradition the eucharist is a domestic liturgy in meal form. This leads us to conclude that from the beginning the church used for the eucharist the dining table and vessels at home rather than the altar and temple vessels for sacrifice. It was largely due to the theology of the eucharist as the *anamnesis* or sacramental memorial of Christ's sacrifice that the church adopted the sacrificial language of the Old Testament: altar, temple, sanctuary, priest. This does not mean that the Jewish or pagan altars, which were normally square structures of stone or marble upon which victims were slain or burnt, were ever introduced into the homes, the *domus ecclesiae*, or the basilicas. Yet in the thinking and language of early theologians the eucharistic table was an altar by extension because upon it the church celebrates the anamnesis of the once-for-all sacrifice of Christ. The great liturgist S. Marsili treats the development of this theological question in his extensive article "Theology of the Eucharistic Celebration."[34] Among the early patristic writers who dealt with the sacrificial nature of the eucharistic meal he names Justin Martyr, Origen, Cyprian, Eusebius of Caesarea, John Chrysostom, Agustine, and Gregory the Great.

What type of vessels did the early church use for the eucharist? It seems that in the first century the eucharistic bread was kept in baskets, since these were the normal bread containers used at home.[35] Matthew 14:20 and John 6:13, which are eucharistic pericopes, speak of twelve *kophínous* or wicker baskets in which the leftovers from the five loaves shared by the crowd were gathered together. One of the frescoes in the catacomb of Callixtus portrays seven baskets containing the eucharistic bread. Wine, on the other hand, was stored in pitchers or jars. These were often earthenware, though some were made of metal. It is likely that communal cups, rather than individual ones, were normally used during family meals. These cups were made from a variety of materials, including glass. The wealthy might own drinking goblets made of precious metals. We can gather from 1 Corinthians 10:16-17 that a communal cup was used during the eucharist in order to underline the unity of the assembly. In short, being a domestic celebration, the eucharist was served in normal house vessels: breadbasket and drinking cup.

By the early third century we learn that wicker baskets were being abandoned for glass and metal patens. Originally patens were dish-shaped vessels large enough to hold loaves of bread. The *Liber Pontificalis* XVI and XVIII, on notices about Pope Zephyrinus and Pope Urban I, informs us that the former made a rule for the church that glass patens should be used for the eucharist, whereas the latter donated twenty-five silver patens.[36] Likewise we are told that Emperor Constantine donated to the Lateran Basilica seven golden patens, each weighing thirty pounds, and sixteen silver patens, each weighing also thirty pounds. *Roman Ordo I* reports that for the fraction at papal Mass the paten was carried by two subdeacons, which seems to suggest that the paten was large and heavy.[37] It is possible that patens from such materials as glass, pottery, and wood continued to be used as late as the eighth century. A curious practice is mentioned by the same *Roman Ordo*: the loaves of bread offered by the faithful were deposited in linen sacks (*sindones* or *saccula*), and at communion the eucharistic bread was again put in linen sacks for distribution to the assembly.[38]

The type of vessel for the wine also underwent evolution. Although the eucharistic cups could be made of glass or ivory—and this continued well into the Middle Ages—by the third century they were increasingly made from precious metals. Some of them might even be decorated with images. The principle of a communal cup would make us believe that the size of the cup was determined by the size of the community. Yet again at the seventh-century papal Mass recorded by *Roman Ordo I* a "main cup" was used, thus implying that there were other cups, probably for the communion of the assembly. In the year 303, in Cirta in North Africa, Munatus Felix, high-priest of the emperor, had the "house where the Christians customarily met" searched. From this account we may surmise that the house was owned by the community, for they customarily met there, and that it was rather amply furnished for worship. Bishop Felix surrendered the possessions of the community, which were mostly for the celebration of the liturgy. The inventory included two golden chalices, six silver chalices, six silver jars, a silver dish, seven silver lamps, two torches, seven short bronze candlesticks, eleven bronze lamps, and several items like tunics and slippers for men and women, presumably for baptism.[39] Surely the church in Cirta could not have been poor by any standard, perhaps because the community was generous in providing expensive vessels for the eucharistic celebration.

We may conclude that the table and vessels used for the eucharist by the early church reflected its theology of the eucharist as the supper of the Lord. Being a meal, it is partaken of by God's family in the setting of a home. The shift from wicker baskets and glass cups to adorned patens and chalices of silver and gold does not at all detract from the original domestic setting of the eucharist. It merely suggests that some communities counted among their members wealthy patrons who donated generously. It also points to the growth of a theological and cultural awareness, which became prevalent from the time of Constantine, that to the dignity of the eucharist corresponds the dignity of a cultic meal.

* * * * * * * *

From the foregoing discussion what clearly emerges is the domestic tradition surrounding the celebration of the eucharist in the early church. The place of celebration was the home or a building that could be transformed into a house where the community could gather to hold the "family" meal. Temples, synagogues, and catacombs did not provide the appropriate space for such a meal. The temple was principally for sacrifices, the synagogue for the word, and the catacombs for the dead. The eucharist, on the other hand, was a meal that was best celebrated at home, according to the apostolic tradition of breaking bread *kat'oikon*, from house to house. Even when the *domus ecclesiae* evolved into the royal basilica, there remained a consciousness that the eucharist was essentially a meal.

We cannot sufficiently stress the importance of the domestic origin and character of the eucharist. It is the context in which the meal aspects of the eucharistic celebration evolved: architectural space for fellowship meal, furnishings and vessels like dining table and cups, music, table blessing or eucharistic prayer, presider. All these components of the celebration point to the domestic nature of the eucharist. This is also the context in which the sacrificial underpinning or content of the eucharist can be best explained. For it is not possible to speak of the eucharist as memorial of Christ's sacrifice outside the ambit of a sacred meal held, not in a temple as part of a sacrificial offering, but in the setting of a home in imitation of Christ's fellowship meals with his disciples. Finally, the domestic character of the eucharist is the church's countercultural message to a world broken by individualism, anonymity, and absence or even denial of family values. In situations like this the image of the church as "family" gathered around the table of the Lord to listen to the word and break the bread in fellowship stands both to accuse the world of its fragmentation and lead it to unity.

It is, of course, true that already in early patristic period the eucharist was regarded as the *anamnesis*, the ritual memorial in the form of a meal, of Christ's unrepeatable and unique sacrifice on the cross. There has always been an awareness that the eucharist was more than a fellowship meal. Christians gathered at home to break bread, but did so in order to recall the mystery of the Lord who offered himself in sacrifice on the cross. By this act of *anamnesis* they experienced the presence of the risen Lord as the word of God was proclaimed, as the bread was broken, as each shared one's faith experience. In a sense they recalled the passion and death of Jesus in their eucharistic assembly, in order to experience his risen presence. That is why the ultimate purpose of the eucharistic celebration is not to recall Christ's sacrificial death through *anamnesis*, but to experience his presence in word, sacrament, and assembly.

But the theology of eucharistic sacrifice successfully imprinted its mark on the thinking and language of early Christian writers. The eucharistic table was increasingly referred to as altar because of its theological association with Calvary. Yet the exterior form of the table remained that of a table for a ritual meal; it was covered with white table cloth as befits a solemn meal. It did not develop into a stone or marble altar for sacrifices in the Jewish or pagan religions, even if at times it might be difficult to recognize it as a dining table. The bread too came to be called "host" from *hostia*, which means sacrificial oblation. For pragmatic reasons it has been reduced to a thin round wafer which hardly corresponds to what people normally call bread. And the presider, whom Justin Martyr called *proëstós*, gradually took the name *sacerdos*, "priest," that is, minister of temple sacrifice. But this linguistic development did not transform the eucharist into a temple sacrifice; it kept its liturgical form as a meal centered on the table blessing and communion.

Likewise the vessels were basically those used at home: bread baskets and drinking cups. The financial resources of the community often dictated the type and quality of the eucharistic vessels: gold patens and cups, or curiously also linen sacks. Though they came in various materials, shapes, sizes, and decor, these vessels alluded to the original domestic setting of the eucharist. The shift from house church to basilicas had surely its effect on the style of celebration. The domestic setting, that "private" character of the eucharist idealized by G. Dix, disappeared, but even in Constantinian basilicas the vessels, for all their imperial quality, were for a meal.

Besides the domestic and meal aspects, language influenced the liturgical shape of the eucharist in the context of the local church's culture. Language expresses a people's cultural patterns; it reveals their hidden thoughts and manifests the values they cherish as a people. The extent and depth of inculturation in the eucharistic liturgy is evident in the language of the prayer formularies and in the rites. For the Roman people of the classical period, culture was defined by their proverbial identifying marks, namely sobriety and rhetoric. These became the identifying marks of most of the Roman eucharistic texts as well. The popes who authored them have succeeded in incorporating into the liturgy the thought and language patterns of the Roman people, that is, those who belonged to the class of the elites and the educated. The language of these prayers is elevated and dignified, but not easily accessible to the rest because of rhetoric. The question that comes to mind is, what kind of language should we use in the liturgy to foster the sense of hospitality, of a welcoming language that can address people across social status and educational attainments? Liturgical language should be a vehicle of unity, not class distinction within the household of God.

The acquired political status of church leaders also profoundly influenced the ceremonial of the eucharistic liturgy in basilicas, especially at the entrance rite, though the rest of the liturgy kept the Roman tradition of sobriety. After the drama of the entrance rite the Mass continued with a simplicity and gravity that seemed to ignore the imperial splendor and magnificence of the basilica. This was especially the case with the liturgy of the eucharist which was marked by austerity. Hence, the core of the eucharist, namely, word and sacrament, retained the original Roman cultural pattern of sobriety and noble simplicity. Or were these the qualities of a domestic celebration that survived the incursion of the imperial court ceremonials?

We can conclude that at an early period the church began to inculturate the eucharistic celebration in the setting of the local people's language, values, dwelling-places, and meal traditions. The key, it seems, for understanding and appreciating this early example of inculturation is the domestic character of the eucharist. Through inculturation the church brought the supper of the Lord to the homes of the faithful.

Notes

1. See J. Jeremias, *The Eucharistic Words of Jesus* (London, 1966); P. Bradshaw, "Zebah Todah and the Origins of the Eucharist," *Ecclesia Orans* 8:3 (1991) 246-260.

2. G. Lathrop offers a fresh insight on the question of Christian sacrifice in his *Holy Things: A Liturgical Theology* (Minneapolis, 1993)

139-158; see also K. Stevenson, *Eucharist and Offering* (New York, 1986) for a fuller treatment of the subject.

3. See S. Marsili, "Teologia della celebrazione dell'eucaristia," in *Anamnesis*, vol 3:2 (Casale Monferrato, 1983) 19-32.

4. G dix, *The Shape of the Liturgy* (London, 1982) 16-35.

5. Ibid.

6. *First Apology* 67, ed. L. Pautigny (Paris, 1904); partial English translation in W. Jurgens, *The Faith of the Early Fathers* (Collegeville, 1970) 57.

7. *Acta Saturnini, Datii* . . ., PL 8:710-711.

8. Dix, *Shape of the Liturgy* 19-35.

9. English text in R. Cabié, *History of the Mass* (Washington, D.C., 1992) 22.

10. J. Boguniowski, *Domus Ecclesiae. Der Ort der Eucharistiefeier in den ersten Jahrhunderten* (Rome, 1986). N. Duval, "L'espace liturgique dans les églises paléochrétiennes." *La Maison-Dieu* 193 (1993) 7-29.

11. R. Cabié, *The Eucharist*, vol. 2 of *The Church at Prayer*, (Collegeville, 1986) 7-123.

12. L. Bouyer, *Liturgy and Architecture* (Notre Dame, 1967) 39-60.

13. W. Huffman and A. Stauffer, *Where We Worship* (Minneapolis, 1987); J. White and S. White, *Church Architecture* (Nashville, 1989); A. Stauffer, "Inculturation and Church Architecture," *Studia Liturgica* 20:1 (1990) 70-80.

14. Cabié, *The Eucharist* 39.

15. *Homily on Jeremiah XIX*, 13, Sources chrétiennes, vol. 238 (1977) 228-230.

16. P. De Clerck, "Le langage liturgique: sa nécessité et ses traits spécifiques," *Questions liturgiques* 73:1-2 (1992) 15-34.

17. C. Vogel, *Medieval Liturgy: Introduction to the Sources* (Washington, D.C. 1986) 294-297; T. Klauser, *A Short History of the Western Liturgy* (Oxford, 1979) 18-24, 37-47.

18. *De Spectaculis*, Corpus Christianorum, vol. 1:1 (1954) 24, p. 248.

19. C. Mohrmann, *Liturgical Latin: Its Origin and Character* (Washington, D.C., 1957).

20. M. Haessly, *Rhetorics in the Sunday Collects of the Roman Missal* (Cleveland, 1938); M. Augé: "Principi di interpetazione dei testi liturgici," *Anamnesis*, vol. 1 (Casale Monferrato, 1979) 159-171.

21. W. Halliwell, *The Style of Pope Leo the Great* (Washington, D.C., 1939); A. Echiegu, *Translating the Collects of the "Sollemnitates Domini" of the "Missale Romanum" of Paul VI in the Language of the African* (Münster, 1984).

22. *Sacramentarium Veronense*, ed. L. Mohlberg (Rome, 1978) 1239, p. 157.

23. E. Bishop, "The Genius of the Roman Rite," *Liturgica Historica* (Oxford, 1918) 1-19.

24. *Le Sacramentaire grégorien*, ed. J. Deshusses (Fribourg, 1971) 36, p. 99.

25. For bibliography and treatment of the Roman Canon see A. Nocent, "La preghiera eucaristica del canone romano," *Anamnesis*, vol. 3:2 (Casale Monferrato, 1983) 229-245; see also E. Mazza, *The Eucharistic Prayers of the Roman Rite* (New York, 1986).

26. Chapter 67, Jurgens 57.

27. *Les Ordines Romani du haut moyen âge*, vol. 2, ed. M. Andrieu (Louvain, 1971) 67-108.

28. A. Chavasse, *La liturgie de la ville de Rome du Ve au VIIIe siècle* (Rome, 1993).

29. L. Duchesne, *Le Liber Pontificalis: Texte, introduction et commentaire* (Paris, 1955) 170-202.

30. Constitutio Constantini, ed. C. Mirbt, *Quellen zur Geschichte des Papstums und des römischen Katholizismus* (Tübingen, 1924) no. 228, pp. 107-112.

31. Klauser, *A Short History* 59-72.

32. R. Berger, "Liturgische Gewänder und Insignien," *Gottesdienst der Kirche*, vol. 3 (Regensburg, 1987) 309-406; Klauser, *A Short History* 32-37.

33. See Lathrop, *Holy Things* 180-203.

34. "Teologia della celebrazione dell'eucaristia," *Anamnesis*, vol. 3:2, 11-186.

35. E. Foley, *From Age to Age: How Christians Celebrated the Eucharist* (Chicago, 1991). The author deals with eucharistic vessels in several parts of the book, which I use gratefully for the information it offers.

36. Duchesne, *Le Liber Pontificalis*, vol. 1, 139 and 143.

37. *Les Ordines Romani du haut moyen âge*, vol. 2, no. 103, p. 100.

38. Ibid. no. 71, p. 91; no. 115, p. 104.

39. Dix, *Shape of the Liturgy* 24-26.

3

The Early Cultural Setting
of Ordination Rites

THE REVISED RITE OF ORDINATION WAS PUBLISHED IN JUNE 1968 AFTER what had been, it seems, a lively discussion by the Consilium. A. Bugnini records both the debate and the details of the work done by the Consilium in his posthumous book *The Reform of the Liturgy 1948-1975*.[1] The most significant change which the Consilium introduced into the rite was the formulary for ordination of the bishop. The sixth-century formulary in the Veronese Sacramentary, until then in unbroken use throughout the Roman Latin Church, was abandoned, and the one in the third-century *Apostolic Tradition* was adopted with minor textual emendations. As regards the presbyteral and diaconal ordinations, the formularies in the Veronese Sacramentary were kept substantially intact, although they underwent considerable textual revision.

The revision of 1989 addressed primarily the ordination formulary for presbyters and the need for a General Introduction, which was lacking in the typical edition of 1968. The second typical edition has certainly made significant improvements on the formulary for presbyters. There remains, however, the lingering uneasiness over the fact that there is no theological and linguistic unity between the formulary for the bishop, which is from the *Apostolic Tradition*, and those for presbyters and deacons, which are basically from the Veronese Sacramentary. They project two different theological visions of the ordained ministry. Thus it takes particular effort, with no clear hope of success, to find a common theological ground for the episcopal ministry, on the one hand, and the presbyteral and diaconal, on the other. Furthermore, the cultural setting and the language of these two sets of formularies are so distant that they cannot be treated as a unit, even from historical and anthropological perspectives. We are dealing, in other words, with two very distinct theological and cultural realities that have been lumped together as a set of ordination rites.

It is not the intention of this study to examine the three formularies of the latest typical edition. This would in reality involve six formularies: three from the *Apostolic Tradition* and three from the Veronese Sacramentary. The aim of this study is more modest, namely to present the cultural setting of the Veronese ordination prayers and how it has, for good or ill, influenced over the centuries the church's vision of ordained ministry. It is one of the attempts of liturgical inculturation whose worth is at least debatable.

THE LANGUAGE OF THE VERONESE
ORDINATION FORMULARIES

The three ordination formularies in the Veronese Sacramentary are in the September *libellus*, which was composed, according to C. Vogel, most probably in the year 558 during the reign of Pope Pelagius I.[2] This date does not, however, exclude the possibility that the formularies antedate the *libellus*. Up until the reform of the ordination rite in 1968, the three formularies had been in use in the Latin Church according to the major recensions found in the Veronese, Gregorian, and Gelasian Sacramentaries and the *Missale Francorum*. Because of serious criticisms made against the formulary for episcopal ordination, Pope Paul VI substituted it with the formulary of the *Apostolic Tradition*.[3] The 1989 rite continues to use the Veronese for the presbyteral formulary (with a good deal of additions) and for the diaconal (with a major omission made in 1968), but it is necessary to examine the episcopal as well, because all three form a theological unit and share the same cultural patterns and language.

Throughout the three formularies certain words borrowed from the socio-political system of the Roman world constantly make their appearance. Notable among them are: *dignitas, honor,* and *gradus* or rank. We may say that the Veronese conception of the three ordination rites as three ascending stages of ecclesiastical ministry has been greatly influenced by this system. To each of these ranks correspond special dignity and honor. There is little doubt that the composer of these formularies regarded the three words "dignity," "honor," and "rank" as the nucleus around which the theology of the three orders and their mutual relationship revolved. D. Power has made a very useful research on the cultural and political origin of these words.[4]

Can we say that this is an example of inculturation that did not work very well? By assimilating the socio-political language of the period and thereby of a certain frame of mind, the Veronese formularies have succeeded in shifting the accent from the shepherding ministry of the *Apostolic Tradition* to the ranking system of Roman society. Alas, the effect of such cultural assimilation lingers on in the thinking and attitude of both clergy and laity.

Dignitas in the socio-political system of the Roman empire denoted the worth or value of a public office as well as the importance of its holder.[5] The word "dignitary" which is still often used in reference to church leaders, is suggestive of this system. In Rome the *dignitas senatoria* pointed to the exalted office of the senator as well as to the person holding that office. We know that in 318 Constantine conferred on bishops civil jurisdiction over court litigations involving Christians. This factor led to the necessity of assigning to them, and to some extent also to presbyters and deacons, a corresponding place in the civil hierarchy.[6]

Thus during the Constantinian era the clergy began to acquire the titles and insignia pertaining to state dignitaries. Bishops, presbyters, and deacons began to be ranked as the ecclesiastical counterparts of civil dignitaries and as such enjoyed the honor and privileges given to state dignitaries. And in situations where the church dominated the political and social scene, it was quite logical that its leaders assumed civil positions and the rights and privileges attached to these positions.

Even today we speak of the dignity of the ordained, a dignity that at times promotes a person to a higher social rank and estimation of the people. In some parts of the world ecclesiastical dignitary and social elite are still quite synonymous. Nevertheless, if it is of any spiritual comfort, the Veronese formularies teach that clerical dignity comes from God who distributes it among the clergy and expects it to be used for God's glory. The formulary for the bishop opens with these words: "God of all honors, God of all the worthy ranks, which serve to your glory in hallowed orders." For presbyters the formulary reads: "Holy Lord, almighty Father, everlasting God, bestower of all the honors and of all worthy ranks which do you service."[7]

Honor is the respect and esteem given by the people to those who hold public office. The title "honorable" and the address "your honor" are connected with the value people and tradition assign to the office. In the thinking of the Veronese it is the consequence of being promoted to a clerical dignity. During the Constantinian era bishops acquired such insignia as were proper to state dignitaries, like the pallium, maniple, miter, and throne, as well as the use of a number of court ceremonials.[8]

The *Donatio Constantini* addresses the clergy with the honorific title of "Reverend" (with its ramifications of Very Reverend, Right Reverend, and Most Reverend): *viris etiam reverendissimis clericis diversi ordinis.*[9] Titles like "His Excellency" and "His Eminence" are residues of the Constantinian socio-political system which the church embraced in the fourth century. They do not necessarily describe the person but rather the office. It is not an easy thing to distinguish the office holder from the office itself. Yet incensation and gestures of reverence, like bowing, are directed to persons, not to the chairs they occupy.

Gradus or rank indicated the various steps a person had to ascend in the course of a public career. One normally moved up from lower to higher ranks, from soldier to emperor. From this cultural milieu we inherited expressions like "ecclesiastical career" and "episcopal promotion." In the Veronese framework the rank of deacons leads to the *potiora*, which can refer to either the presbyterate or the episcopate. As the formulary for deacons augurs, "by fitting advancements (*successus*) from a lower rank may [they] be worthy through your grace to take up higher things." The author of the Veronese formularies regards the three orders in ascending ranks: diaconate, presbyterate, and episcopate. The word *ordo* itself, which belonged not to the religious vocabulary of ancient Rome but to its civil institutions, designated the clergy as a group distinct from the faithful.[10] In the fourth century the *ordo ecclesiasticus* was an established institution recognized by imperial decree. Tertullian, in his typical bravura, had remarked earlier that "it was by church authority that a distinction is now made between order and people."[11]

In imitation of the Roman system the clergy was organized according to rank. Each rank was defined by corresponding dignity and honors. Thus at an early stage ecclesiastical ministry was already viewed from the Roman socio-political institution. Church ministers formed a group distinct from the people they served. The Roman *senatus populusque* found its counterpart in the church's *ordo populusque*, the hierarchy and the faithful. The concept of pastoral ministry or shepherding was surely not abandoned, but it was expressed in the socio-political language and insignia of ancient Rome. The word "order" itself stressed that aspect of ministry which has always stood prominently in church hierarchy: the function of governing, which is but one of the functions of the clergy. The offices of preaching and sanctifying are not contained in this secular word, except by force of usage. In other words, when we refer to church ministry as order, we unwittingly preserve a fourth-century cultural setting.

THE VERONESE FORMULARY FOR THE
ORDINATION OF BISHOPS

In the Veronese formularies for ordination, culture and theology are so closely allied, that the study of one needs to be supplemented by the other. When we examine the cultural elements of these texts, we are constrained to take a good look at the theology they contain. In the Veronese formularies, culture and theology are in constant dialogue, because in them the theological content of ordination is vested in the cultural form of the Roman system.

The opening line of the ordination formulary for the bishop sets the tone of the entire composition: *Deus honorum omnium, Deus omnium dignitatum*, "God of all the honors, God of all the worthy ranks."[12] These and related words or phrases are constant elements of the series of the Veronese ordination formularies. They remind the candidates for orders that God is the source of all honor and the bestower of every dignity. Honor and dignity describe the sacramental orders and consequently the class of persons who receive them. However, such qualities are not conferred for the personal gratification of those who are raised to this class. Rather, the bishop is under obligation to serve (the Latin is *famulari*) for the glory of the bestower. The same thought appears in the ordination prayer for presbyters. These are also exhorted to do battle (the Latin is *militare*) for the glory of God. Though these formularies lavishly employ the socio-political terminology of the period and are built on the concepts of dignity, honor, and rank, they nevertheless make a considerable attempt to sublimate them: the dignity of holy orders comes from God and gives God glory.

Like most of the liturgical formularies for blessing and consecration, the ordination prayer for the bishop turns to the Old Testament for typology. In the liturgy biblical types have the distinct role of rooting the reality of the church in salvation history. Their use reveals a desire to show the continuity between the Old Testament and the present dispensation. Biblical typology is the liturgical way of affirming that God's plan as set out in the history of the chosen people has been fulfilled in Christ and the church. The problem, of course, is that the practice of invoking Old Testament priestly types easily leads to the assimilation of the theological and linguistic components of such types. The temptation always existed of viewing the ordained ministries of the New Testament in the light of the Aaronic priesthood. Not rarely did theology and practice succumb to it.[13]

The Old Testament type for episcopal ordination is the anointing of Aaron as high priest. The latter part of the prayer alludes to this: "Hallow them with the dew of heavenly unction. May it flow down, O Lord, richly upon their head; may it run down below the mouth, may it go down to the uttermost parts of the whole body." However, what caught the interest of the author of this text, who seemed to have greatly delighted in it, was the episcopal vesture. The greater part of the formulary is a catechesis on it or, one might rightly say, an apology. At his ordination the bishop, particularly of Rome, donned the imperial robes and wore the insignia of his exalted office. Our author felt that this needed to be explained.

The explanation is not historical but typological. In a conversation with Moses on cult, God made a decree regarding the priestly vesture of Aaron. Leviticus 8 mentions tunic, girdle, robe, ephod, pectoral containing the Urim and the Thummim, and turban with the golden plate. The description surely did not fit the episcopal vesture; the bishop did not dress like an Old Testament high priest. Instead of seeking explanation from the imperial dress code of the period, the author of this Veronese formulary had recourse to the Aaronic era. During the sacred rites Aaron was to wear "a mystical robe." This, our author explains, was a foreshadowing of the spiritual adornment of bishops: "the dignity of robes no longer commends to us the pontifical glory, but the splendor of spirits." Likewise "the radiance of gold, the sparkling of jewels, the variety of diverse workmanship" that surrounded the person of Aaron are now to show forth in the conduct and deeds of the bishops.

Thus the Veronese formulary has developed the biblical type of the episcopal office on the basis chiefly of the priestly insignia of Aaron. What the bishop wore at his ordination had not the slightest similarity with the Aaronic vesture, in the same way that the New Testament priesthood has nothing to do with that of the Old Testament, but this did not seem to have bothered the author. As far as the author was concerned the episcopal garments and insignia were symbols of priestly office; they had been prefigured by the priestly robes of Aaron. Although by their cultural origin they signified the function of governing, biblical typology has imposed on them a new meaning, the office of priesthood.

The second part of the ordination prayer, the epiclesis proper, reads: "Complete the fullness of your mystery (*mysterii tui summam*) in your priests, and equipped with all the adornments of glory, hallow them with the dew of heavenly unction (*caelestis unguenti fluore*)." The formulary describes the episcopate as "the fullness of God's mystery," and our theology has translated this as "the fullness of priesthood." But what catches our interest here is the word *summa*, which is more adequately rendered by "highest point" than by "fullness" which is the equivalent of the Latin *plenitudo*. As the substantive superlative of *superus*, it alludes to heights more than to plenitude or completeness. In this context we have reason to regard the phrase *mysterii summa* as another way of saying that the episcopate is the highest rank in God's appointed structure of authority. In short, underneath its typology and theology we can perceive the cultural milieu of the Roman civilization. The episcopate is the *summus gradus*, although the formulary wants us to understand this as the antitypal fulfillment of Aaron's supreme priesthood. The dialogue between theology and culture is perhaps nowhere as visible as here.

To reinforce the priestly character of the episcopate over its cultural and socio-political conditioning, the formulary asks further that the bishop be "hallowed with the dew of heavenly unction." It will be recalled that in Leviticus 8:12 Moses poured the chrism on the head of Aaron, consecrating him by unction, after he had been vested as high priest. Our formulary seems to refer to this, when it pictures the bishop as "equipped with all the adornments of glory," like Aaron at the time of his anointing. But we may suspect that such "adornments of glory," like the "pontifical glory," described more the imperial robes worn by the bishop at his ordination than the priestly vesture of Aaron. Yet it would appear that our author was intent on severing the ties of the ordination rites with the Constantinian socio-political system by ignoring them and focusing his attention instead on biblical types.

As regards the *unguentum* or unction, it is quite sure that it does not imply corporal anointing, which was unknown in the fifth-century Roman rite of episcopal ordination.[14] It was only by the middle of the eighth century that bishops of the Gallican tradition were anointed, following the practice of anointing the Frankish kings. The Veronese, on the other hand, gives to *unguentum* a mystical or metaphorical interpretation. It is the action of the Holy Spirit who fills the candidate with power. This is developed in the third part of the formulary: "May it flow down, O Lord, richly upon their head; may it run down below the mouth; may it go down to the uttermost parts of the whole body, so that the power of the Holy Spirit may both fill them within and surround them without." The allusion to Psalm 133 is obvious: "Fine as oil on the head, running down the beard, running down Aaron's beard to the collar of his robes." Thus, in contrast with "adornments of glory" which evoke the imperial vesture, the phrase "dew of heavenly unction" refers to the anointing of Aaron unto priesthood, though its actual practice was inspired in later centuries by the anointing of kings.

The other petition refers to the leadership and authority of the bishop: "Grant to them an episcopal throne (*cathedram episcopalem*) to rule your church and entire people." The episcopal throne symbolizes the bishop's office of ruler. By association with the academic *cathedra* it has come to symbolize specifically the leadership he exercises through teaching, through the preaching of the word. Thus, in a transferred sense the episcopal throne can represent the principal ministry of the bishop, namely preaching. It is odd that the Veronese formulary makes no suggestion regarding his eucharistic ministry or pastoral care. In passing, it might be useful to recall that one of the privileges granted by Constantine to Pope Sylvester and to his successors was the use of the throne. This was one of the insignia attached to the power of jurisdiction given to bishops in civil matters involving Christians.[15] Thus the *cathedra episcopalis*, though it indicates today spiritual leadership in the church, especially through the preaching of the word, was originally a symbol of civil authority.

The phrase "entire people" (*plebs universa*) has an interesting textual history. For the sake of precision the Pontifical of the Roman Curia changed it to "people committed to his care" (*plebs sibi commissa*) for bishops other than the pope, but retained it for the bishop of Rome. It is obvious that the Pontifical understood *plebs universa* to mean *ecclesia universalis*, and hence could not attribute it to other bishops. However, it seems that, as used by the formulary, it means nothing more than all the faithful of a local church for which the bishop is ordained. The Veronese formulary, which is in the plural, could be used for bishops other than the pope. Although the bishop of Rome is head of the universal church, this doctrine does not get strong support in this ordination formulary.[16]

Both J. Lécuyer and A. Santantoni sharply criticize the Veronese ordination formulary for bishops. J. Lécuyer laments that its typology says nothing about the essential meaning of the ordination rite, except that the bishop should, in a spiritual context, mirror in himself the glory of the high priest Aaron. A. Santantoni, on the other hand, enumerates the defects of the formulary. Two of these are: the lack of reference to the principal tasks of the bishop, especially preaching, and failure to mention Christ's anointing by the Holy Spirit, which is the New Testament type. Santantoni has, however, overlooked the possible implication of *cathedra* for the episcopal office of preaching.[17] A. Bugnini records how the Consilium viewed the Veronese formulary: "The Roman part develops a single theme: the bishop is the high priest of the new covenant. As Aaron was consecrated by an anointing with oil and the donning of vestments, so the bishop is constituted high priest by a spiritual anointing and the adornment of virtue. All this is true, but excessively scanty now that we have the teaching of Vatican II on the episcopate. Nothing is said of apostolic succession, and almost nothing of the episcopal office, except for the words 'Grant him the episcopal chair'."[18] Such pointed criticisms, however, need be contextualized. Working on the imperial insignia as point of departure, the composer of the Veronese formulary could construct only an extremely limited theology of the episcopate, even with the assistance of biblical typology. One might even ask whether, after all, the main interest of the composer was theology.

Given these defects, the Consilium made an attempt to revise the text, but this proved futile. In the end it decided to adopt the formulary of the *Apostolic Tradition* which it perceived as a richer theological statement on the episcopate.

THE VERONESE FORMULARY FOR THE ORDINATION OF PRESBYTERS

The literary style and vocabulary of the formulary for the ordination of presbyters point to the author of the formulary for bishops. It employs the same socio-political language of the period. Words like *dignitas, honor,* and *gradus* are so entrenched in the thought pattern of the formulary that they influence its theological outlook. It is difficult to present the theology of the presbyterate in this formulary without recourse to its vocabulary and the underpinning socio-political system. It might be useful also to note that this formulary actually forms one theological and linguistic unit with those for bishops and deacons.

The ordination formulary is introduced by a bidding prayer "that upon these his servants, whom he has chosen for the office of presbyter (*ad presbyterii munus*)" God may multiply heavenly gifts. The prayer that follows defines what these heavenly gifts are. They are the benediction of the Holy Spirit and the power (*virtus*) of priestly grace. The ordination formulary itself begs God to renew in the person being ordained the Spirit of holiness. A point of interest here is the phrase *presbyterii munus*, the office to which the candidate is being raised. In the Roman system *munus* referred to public office, as in *reipublicae munus* or *consulare munus*. In accord with this system the church adopted the word to signify the public office held by bishops, presbyters, and deacons.[19] In short, *presbyterii munus* means that the presbyter is a public official of the church.

Another point of interest is the phrase *gratiae sacerdotalis* or priestly grace. With this the bidding prayer declares that the presbyterate is a sacerdotal or priestly rank. The ordination formulary itself refers to it as one of the two *sacerdotales gradus* prefigured in the old dispensation. The use of this Old Testament type leaves no room for doubt as to the author's concept of the presbyterate as possessing a priestly character.[20] In the author's thinking a person is raised to the *presbyterii munus* in order to exercise priestly functions. Thus the older concept of presbyter as an elder of a synagogal community with the function of counselor gave way to the temple priesthood whose concern were the sacrifices. Whereas the presbyter was associated with synagogal ministry, the priest was assigned to the temple liturgy. Now the presbyter takes over the function of priests and his public office is identified with it.[21]

The medieval liturgical documents, however, have generally kept the ancient nomenclature of "ordination to the presbyterate." Thus the twelfth-century Roman Pontifical continues to speak of the candidate *qui presbyter ordinandus est*, except in codex 570 of Lyons, where it shifts to *ordinandus in sacerdotem*, and in the codices B of the British Museum and the Vatican C 631 and O 270, where it uses *ordo sacerdotalis* for a description of the tasks of presbyters, like "offering acceptable sacrifices for sins."[22] The thirteenth-century Pontifical of Durand retains the "Ordination of a Presbyter," but speaks of *indumenta sacerdotalia* or priestly vestments.[23] It is in the Pontifical of the Roman Curia where the word *sacerdos* is more consistently used both during the rite of ordination and for the liturgical vestments of presbyters.[24] What

\

is remarkable in all these stages of development is that the pontificals down to our time never departed from the traditional title of the ordination rite: it is always called "Ordination to the Presbyterate."

The formulary of ordination opens with the now familiar words: "Holy Lord, almighty Father, everlasting God, bestower of all the honors and of all worthy ranks (*dignitatum*) which do you service (*militant*).[25] This introductory invocation considers the presbyterate an honor and a worthy rank in the ecclesiastical hierarchy. This manner of speaking, as we pointed out earlier, was influenced by the socio-political system of the period. But here as in the other formularies the author overlays the secular element with spiritual meaning: the honor and dignity of the presbyterate proceed from God, and the person who receives the order of the presbyterate must use such honor and dignity for the service of God. The English "service" is an inadequate rendering of the Latin *militia*. In Roman usage this word denoted the service rendered by soldiers or public officials to the state. Here it suggests that the presbyterate is a form of *militia* in the service of God. The sixth-century Rule of St. Benedict applies the term to the monk who wished to do battle for Christ the King through the weapons of obedience: *Domino Christo vero regi militaturus.*[26]

After the opening invocation the formulary praises God for perfecting and sustaining the universe and for making the human race increase and develop in accord with the divine wise disposition. By divine providence God established the different ranks of ministers arranged in due order (*per ordinem dispositum*) for the benefit of rational nature.[27] This looks like a philosophical construct of God's plan, but underlying it is clearly the notion of the Roman socio-political system whereby public offices and services were arranged according to rank. On this premise the author develops the biblical types of the presbyterate to illustrate its nature and its place in God's providential design as a second rank. If the formulary for the bishop concentrates on pontifical splendor and glory, the formulary for presbyters focuses on ranks.

From the "due order" willed by God "the priestly ranks (*sacerdotales gradus*) and the offices of the levites arose." This is the first biblical type, namely the Old Testament ranks of high priests and priests and the rank of levites. Our Veronese formulary calls them *sacramenta mystica*, that is, foreshadowings of the New Testament ranks of bishop, presbyters, and deacons. When God appointed high priests to rule over the people, God also chose to be their companions and helpers "men of a lesser order and secondary dignity" (*sequentis ordinis et secundae dignitatis*). It is both amazing and amusing how the Roman system of socio-political ranks has been applied to the Old Testament priesthood. But it is a necessary measure to bring the biblical type closer to its Christian antitype: both can now be viewed from the same cultural context. The sense of the biblical type is obvious: in the priestly hierarchy bishops belong to the first order and possess the highest dignity, whereas presbyters occupy the second place. At their ordination presbyters are raised to the priestly dignity of the second rank.

We noted that the ranking system is entrenched in the Veronese theology of the presbyterate. The widespread presence of the following phrases in the text confirms this: *sequens ordo, secunda dignitas, secundi praedicatores, secundi meriti munus*. The office of presbyters is insistently spoken of as second in respect of the office of the bishop to whom they are helpers (*adiumenta*) and colleagues or fellow-workers (*cooperatores ordinis nostri*).[28] The role of presbyters as assistants is given urgency by the bishop's own confession: "Wherefore on our weakness also, we beseech you, O Lord, bestow these assistants, for we who are so much frailer need so many more."

The Veronese formulary offers two other Old Testament types of the Christian presbyterate, namely Moses and the seventy elders, and Aaron and his sons. As the seventy elders were chosen to be assistants (*adiutoribus*) to Moses in his task of governing the countless multitudes in the desert, presbyters have been instituted to assist the bishop. It was through those seventy elders that God "spread out the spirit of Moses in the desert," as Numbers 11:16-17 narrates, so that Moses could govern the people with greater ease.[29] It is not clear whether the Veronese formulary interprets *Mose spiritus* as the person of the Holy Spirit or as a kind of spiritual power which Moses possessed. What matters in the end is the typological doctrine that the presbyters share the "spirit of the bishop" in their capacity as colleagues and assistants to him. Being second in rank, they derive from the higher rank their authority to govern the people.

The other Old Testament type presents Eleazar and Ithamar, the two sons of Aaron, the high priest. To them God imparted the "richness of their father's plenty" (*paternae plenitudinis abundantiam*). The type is drawn from Leviticus 8 which describes the priestly consecration of Aaron and his two sons. Though they were not high priests like their father, they enjoyed in abundance the fullness of his priestly office. What this seems to indicate, at least as far as the priestly functions were concerned, is that the priests shared the duties and privileges of the high priest in offering salutary sacrifices in the temple and performing all the other liturgical acts described in Leviticus 9, or as our author explains, "so that the benefit (*meritum*) of priests might be sufficient for the salutary sacrifices and the rites of a more frequent worship." The Latin *meritum* stands for military service, and the *stipendia meritorum* is the salary thereof. It seems therefore that *meritum sacerdotum* should be translated "priestly service" rather than "benefit." What the phrase means is that the sufficient number of priests would ensure an unhampered service in the temple. We note how the author has employed once again a Roman technical term in the context of the Old Testament.

Applying such biblical typology to presbyters, our formulary affirms the priestly character of the presbyteral rank. In suggesting that presbyters share in the "richness of the bishop's plenty," it does not obviously allow us to conclude that by ordination presbyters acquire the same rank as the bishop. This would totally undermine the Veronese principle of diversification of ecclesiastical ministry by ranks. What it seems to tell us is that presbyters share in their capacity of assistants the priestly functions of the bishop, even if tradition has reserved some of these functions to the bishop. Presiding at the eucharist and delivering the homily and administering confirmation, penance, and the nuptial blessing used to be an episcopal reserve.

The Veronese presents biblical types for presbyters not only from the Old Testament; it also draws from the New Testament. God assigned companions (*comites*) to the Apostles, meaning the Twelve (Lk 9:1-5). The word *comites*, usually in the plural, referred to the retinue that accompanied a Roman magistrate or the imperial court itself. In this formulary who were the *comites*? They could be the seventy disciples whom Jesus himself appointed to preach and heal, as we read in Luke 10:1-11, or the elders whom the Apostles instituted to take charge of every community they had established, as Acts 14:23 informs us.[30] In our text they are called "teachers of the faith" and, more precisely, "secondary preachers" (*secundi praedicatores*).[31] The message of this New Testament type is clear. Presbyters are chosen by God to assist the bishop in his function as teacher. They too are teachers of the faith; they too exercise the office of preaching in the church. But they perform this task as secondary ministers, as assistants to the bishop to whom the office of preaching primarily belongs. According to this typology, the bishop represents the twelve Apostles, while the presbyters represent the seventy disciples in Luke or the elders in Acts.

The foregoing biblical types reveal the theological thinking of the author regarding the office of presbyters. Bishops are compared to Moses (office of government), to Aaron (office of sanctification), and to the Apostles (office of preaching). It is in the context of this threefold episcopal office that presbyters are ordained: they assist the bishop in the government of the church, in his ministry of sanctification through the liturgy, and in his mission of preaching the word. However, we should not lose sight of the cultural setting in which this theological reflection took place. The influence of the Roman ranking system on the Veronese formulary cannot be easily ignored.

The heart of the entire prayer is the epiclesis, which according to Pope Paul VI constitutes the form of the sacrament: "Grant, we beseech you, Father, the dignity of the presbyterate (*presbyterii dignitatem*) to these your servants . . ."[32] Further down the text, the phrase "office of second dignity" (*secundi meriti munus*) explains the office of presbyters in relation to that of the bishop. What the Veronese prays for is that the candidates be raised to the second rank of church hierarchy. It is rather astonishing that two phrases from the Roman socio-political system form part of the most solemn part of the ordination formulary. Indeed they define the nature of the presbyteral office as an ecclesiastical dignity second only to the episcopal rank. One might find this theologically too narrow a view of the presbyterate. Is this all

there is to say about the nature of this sacrament? If one works—
as the author of our formulary did—with a zeal approaching
obsession, on the basis of a cultural premise like the Roman, the
answer is evidently in the affirmative. This is one weakness of
the process and methodology of this type of inculturation,
wherein cultural patterns are incorporated wholesale into the
liturgy, even granting that they are given a truly biblical
reinterpretation.

What might be useful to note at this point is that the formulary speaks of ordination to the rank of the presbyterate, not to
the office of priesthood. Surely in consideration of the Old Testament priestly typology it is quite clear that our text assigns
"priestly" ministry to presbyters and directs us to acknowledge
this. Yet the expression "ordination to the priesthood" is not
exact, because it confuses the ecclesiastical rank with the priestly
function that is common to both bishops and priests. At any
rate, the liturgical tradition has consistently called the rite "Ordination to the Presbyterate." Unfortunately the English language has been remiss in the use of the word "priest," when it
intends the technical and more appropriate word "presbyter."

The epiclesis invokes the gift of the Holy Spirit: "Renew in
their inward parts the Spirit of holiness." Being the object of an
epiclestic prayer, the Spirit here should be understood to refer to
the third person of the Trinity. The clumsy English phrase "inward parts" translates the Latin Vulgate's *viscera* in Psalm 50.
The naming of the Spirit as the Spirit of holiness, rather than
Holy Spirit, was probably influenced by the author's priestly
approach to the presbyteral ministry. Presbyters, like the Old
Testament priests, have the duty to be holy, to show forth in
their life the pattern of all righteousness (*censura morum*) and the
example of daily conversion (*conversatio*). Furthermore they are
to "render a good account of the stewardship entrusted to them"
by fulfilling their task of sanctification. For all this they need the
Spirit of holiness.

In conclusion and on the basis of the formulary we have
examined, we may affirm that one is ordained to be presbyter,
though this implies "priestly" functions for which he receives
the Spirit of holiness. The identity of the presbyter consists in
living out the implications of being a presbyter, of being shep-
herd, *leitourgos*, and teacher. This the presbyter does with deep

consciousness that the particular order to which he belongs is second in rank and dignity, that is, it is exercised in relation to the office of the bishop. In this text we note how profoundly culture has influenced theological thought, and how success-fully theology has imposed a Christian dimension upon the Roman socio-political system.

THE VERONESE FORMULARY FOR THE ORDINATION OF DEACONS

The diaconate ranks third in church hierarchy. The Veronese formulary merely refers to it as the "lower rank" (*inferior gradus*) among the "three ranks (*trinos gradus*) of ministers." It is rather surprising that it never calls it "third rank," although it repeat-edly reminds the presbyters that in the life of the church their role is second to that of the bishop. The language of this formu-lary, like the one for the bishop and the presbyters, is grafted on the system of the period which focuses on ranks and honor.

What role does the Veronese assign to deacons? The bidding prayer begs that those whom God has called to the office of the diaconate (*officium diaconii*) may be filled with heavenly bless-ing. In this formulary the word *officium* has practically the same meaning as *munus*, which in this set of Veronese formularies signifies the liturgical ministry of the ordained. Thus, we may understand this text as denoting the liturgical character of the diaconate.[33] This appears to be the mind of the author, as we can gather from the bidding prayer. In the light of the Old Testa-ment typology, our text goes so far as to call the office of deacons "the office of levites." Just as the levites were appointed to serve at the temple altar, so "may [the deacons] rightly fulfill the ministry of the holy altar." Though nothing is said explicitly about the eucharistic liturgy, this is implied in the word "altar." At this point in time the shift from the table service rendered by deacons to the altar ministry performed by levites seems have been securely established.

The ordination prayer itself opens with a lengthy praise of God, the "giver of honors, distributor of orders, and bestower of offices." God renews all things through Jesus Christ whose body, the church, God adorns with a "variety (*varietas*) of heav-enly graces." Yet God unites (*unitas*) the church wondrously in a single structure. Variety in honors, orders, and offices finds unity of purpose in the growth of God's temple, that is, God's people. When God in divine providence established "the service of the sacred office in three ranks of ministers," God's intention was to foster the increment of the temple. The mention of temple sets the stage for the role deacons are to play in the plan of salvation. Like the levites of old who "remained in faithful vigilance over the mystical working of [God's] house," the deacons are ordained "to serve in [God's] sanctuaries." This merely reaffirms the priestly character the Veronese attributes to the hierarchy: bishops and presbyters exercise a priestly office, and deacons minister to them. Though deacons are not the priests bishops and presbyters are, they operate within the priestly ambit.

Throughout the formulary the only biblical type assigned to deacons are the levites. In Numbers 3:6-9 the tribe of Levi is appointed to serve Aaron and his sons. The tribe is also given charge of the furnishings of the tent of meeting and of ministering at the tabernacle. The Veronese calls tasks "mystical workings." They prefigure the office of deacons who, like the levites, are to serve in God's sanctuary (*sacrariis servituros*). It seems that ministry in the sanctuary defines the nature of the *officium diaconii*. Considering the Veronese conception of the eucharist as a sacrificial offering, the references to levites and the temple point clearly to the eucharistic ministry of deacons. Doubtless there are other diaconal tasks, but our text, which offers no other biblical type, confines the ministry of deacons to the eucharist.[34]

As in the presbyteral ordination, where the bishop makes an apology about his weakness and frailty, we read here a similar apology: "Being men we are ignorant of divine thought and highest reason, we judge their [deacons'] life as best we can." Those who elected the deacons may fail in their judgment, but God knows the depth of each person's heart. This part of the text, which is clearly apologetic in tone, seems to indicate that at this time the clergy alone, and no longer the people, chose the candidates for holy orders. In fact the *Missale Francorum* directs the bishop to ask the people to confirm his choice of candidates to the diaconate.[35] Did this practice emerge from a felt need within the church to counteract the growing interference of political power in the question of appointment to ecclesiastical offices?

The epiclesis is the heart of this Veronese prayer: "Send upon them, Lord, we beseech you, the Holy Spirit, by whom, faithfully accomplishing the work of ministry, they may be strengthened with the gift of your sevenfold grace." Of the three formularies for ordination this alone has the distinction of asking explicitly for the descent of the Holy Spirit on the candidate. The one for the bishop prays that the "fullness of God's mystery" be completed in his priests, whereas the one for presbyters focuses on the elevation of the candidates to the second rank of the hierarchy.

What is meant here by "sevenfold grace"? The number seven can signify the abundance of God's grace or quite simply the grace of the Holy Spirit which is conferred upon deacons to strengthen them in their ministry.[36] But the number seven can also refer to the seven virtues named by our formulary, virtues the deacons are expected to cultivate, namely discreet authority, constant modesty, purity of innocence, observance of spiritual discipline, example of chastity, testimony of good conscience, and perseverance. It is interesting to note that the 1989 revision has substituted *castitatis exemplo* with *conversationis exemplo*, an ancient expression which signifies the daily conversion of one's life and values. The formulary for presbyters requires them to acquire this virtue, and the Rule of St. Benedict includes it among the monastic vows. Although chastity is a virtue every Christian whether clerical or lay should nurture, it is possible that the 1989 modification of the Veronese text was motivated by the ordination of married men to the diaconate. At any rate, *conversatio* has a broader and richer meaning than chastity.

We come to a final consideration. Our formulary concludes with the prayer that "by fitting advancements from a lower rank [the deacons] may be worthy through your grace to take up higher things (*potiora*)." This is a declaration that the diaconate is a transitional rank. The idea is not a Veronese novelty. We come across the Ethiopic version of *Apostolic Tradition* which also considers the diaconate as a transitional stage to *gradum maioris ordinis*, supposing of course that this text is earlier than the Veronese.[37]

Nowhere is the influence of the socio-political system of rank promotion as dominant and incisive as in this part of the Veronese formulary. Surely the practice of transitional diaconate need not be blamed on the Roman system of that era, but we cannot deny that the language employed to explain the practice has been borrowed directly from that particular system. Since the order of deacons is a lower rank, whereas the orders of presbyters and bishops are higher, the diaconate becomes logically a passage to the higher and more exalted ranks of the hierarchy. A change came about dramatically with the revision of this formulary in 1968. The reference to advancement from lower to higher ranks was dropped from the text. In his Apostolic Constitution *Pontificalis Romani* Pope Paul VI explained that the elimination had been motivated by the reestablishment in the Latin Church of the permanent diaconate. Perhaps it is never too late to correct the errors of the past.

* * * * * * * *

From the point of view of good methodology it is clear that we cannot examine one formulary for ordination without due regard for the other two with which it forms a theological and linguistic unit. The episcopate, presbyterate, and diaconate are so intertwined, that we cannot extricate one from the other, as if they had been merely juxtaposed. They were created together, they grew together, indeed they were built on each other. The kind of theology we have regarding bishops will necessarily influence our thinking on the presbyterate and diaconate. In other words, we should avoid doing theology on the Veronese formularies for presbyters and deacons independently of the corresponding formulary for the bishop, even if the 1968 reform chose to substitute it with another text. It makes little or no sense to speak of the *secundi meriti munus* or "office of second rank" which presbyters receive in ordination outside of that general vision of the Veronese Sacramentary in which the bishop holds the "office of the highest rank," and the deacon the "office of the lowest rank." In short, whether we deal with the *Apostolic Tradition* or the Veronese Sacramentary, we should take into account the theological, cultural, and linguistic patterns found in these two sets of ordination formularies.

Notes

1. A. Bugnini, *The Reform of the Liturgy 1948-1975* (Collegeville, 1990) 707-723. For a detailed treatment of the preconciliar discussions leading to the conciliar reform of Constitution on the Sacred Liturgy, see J. Joncas, "Recommendations Concerning Roman Rite Ordinations Leading to the Reform Mandated in *Sacrosanctum Concilium* 76," *Ecclesia Orans* 9:3 (1992) 307-339.

2. *Sacramentarium Veronense*, ed. L. Mohlberg (Rome, 1978) XXVII, nos. 947 (for bishops), 951 (for presbyters), and 954 (for deacons); see C. Vogel, *Medieval Liturgy: An Introduction to the Sources* (Washington D.C., 1986) 40.

3. See J. Lécuyer, "La prière d'ordination de l'évêque," *Nouvelle revue théologique* 89 (1967) 601-606.

4. D.N. Power, *Ministers of Christ and His Church* (London, 1969).

5. For treatment of the words "dignity," "honor," and "rank" as well as those related to them, see Power, *Ministers of Christ and His Church*; P. Jounel, "Ordinations," in *The Church at Prayer*, vol. 3 (Collegeville, 1988) 139-141.

6. T. Klauser, *A Short History of the Western Liturgy* (Oxford, 1979) 32-37.

7. For the English translation of these Veronese formularies, see P. Bradshaw's adaptation of H. Porter's *Ordination Rites of the Ancient Churches of East and West* (New York, 1990) 215-218.

8. T. Klauser: "Bischöfe auf dem Richterstuhl," *Jahrbuch für Antike und Christentum* 5 (Münster, 1962) 129-174;

9. *Liber Pontificalis*, vol. 1, ed. L. Duchesne (Paris, 1955) 139.

10. See P. van Beneden, *Aux origines d'une terminologie sacramentelle: ordo, ordinare, ordinatio dans la littérature chrétienne avant 313* (Louvain, 1974).

11. *De Exhortatione Castitatis* 7, 3, Corpus Christianorum, vol. 2, 1024-1025.

12. The English translator preferred to use "ranks" for *dignitates*. Rank refers more to *gradus*.

13. For a more detailed treatment of the Old Testament types used in ordination formularies, see B. Botte, "L'ordre d'après les prières d'ordination," *Etudes sur le sacrement de l'ordre* (Paris, 1957) 13-35; P. Gy, "Le théologie des prières anciennes pour l'ordination des évêques et des prêtres," *Revue des sciences philosophiques et théologiques* 58 (1974) 599-618.

14. See Bradshaw, *Ordination Rites of the Ancient Churches* 18.

15. *Liber Pontificalis*, vol. 1, 139; T. Klauser, "Bischöfe auf dem Richterstuhl" 129-174.

16. See A. Santantoni, *L'Ordinazione episcopale* (Rome, 1976) 59-6; but see also J. Lécuyer, "La prière d'ordination de l'évêque," *Nouvelle révue théologique* 89 (1967) 602-603.

17. Lécuyer, "La prière d'ordination de l'évêque" 601-602; Santantoni, *Ordinazione episcopale* 61.

18. Bugnini, *The Reform of the Liturgy 1948-1975* 714.

19. See B. Botte, "Secundi meriti munus," *Questions liturgiques et paroissiales* 21 (1936) 84-88.

20. For the influence of the Old Testament priestly types on Christian thinking, see P. Gy, "Remarques sur le vocabulaire antique du sacerdoce chrétien," *Etudes sur le sacrament de l'ordre* (Paris, 1957) 125-145; B. Botte: "L'ordre d'après les prières d'ordination," ibid. 13-35. B. Botte writes that the use of the word "priest" in these Veronese formularies does not allow us to think of bishops and presbyters as some kind of Roman priests of antiquity or of Old Testament priests. Christian priesthood, he explains, belongs to another category which is charismatic and spiritual.

21. We should note, however, that the *Apostolic Tradition*, no. 8, distinguishes the diaconate from the episcopate and presbyterate, when it says that unlike them the deacon is not ordained *in sacerdotium*.

22. *Le Pontifical romain au moyen-âge*, vol. 1, ed. M. Andrieu (Vatican City, 1972) 131, 134, and 137.

23. *Le Pontifical romain au moyen-âge*, vol. 3 (Vatican City, 1973) 366, 368, 373, and 520.

24. *Le Pontifical romain au moyen-âge*, vol. 2 (Vatican City, 1973) 339, 343, and 346.

25. The 1989 revision did away with this socio-political category. The Veronese phrase *honorum omnium et omnium dignitatum* is now made to read *humanae dignitatis auctor* (see Vatican II's Declaration on Religious Freedom, no. 1) *et distributor omnium gratiarum* (see 1 Cor 12:4). See the comparative table of the formularies of 1968 and 1989 in *Notitiae* 283 (1990) 116-121. The table shows the variations and the sources both biblical and conciliar, particularly *Lumen Gentium* and *Presbyterorum Ordinis*. See P. Tena, "La Prex Ordinationis de los presbiteros en la II Edicion Tipica," ibid. 126-133.

26. *The Rule of St. Benedict*, Prologue (Collegeville, 1981)

27. The revision of 1989 adds a statement regarding one of the ministries of the presbyterate: *ad efformandum populum sacerdotalem*, to build up a priestly people. The theological concern here is the relationship that should exist between ordained ministry and the common priesthood.

28. The part of the Veronese formulary that underwent major revision in 1989 is where the functions of presbyters are enumerated. New

elements were introduced in order to be more explicit about the meaning of *probi cooperatores ordinis nostri*. The added elements are: 1) preaching the gospel; 2) celebration of the sacraments, particularly baptism, eucharist, reconciliation, and care of the sick; and 3) prayer for the people.

29. The text is somewhat difficult to interpret; see G. Ferraro, *Le preghiere di ordinazione al diaconato, al presbiterato, e all'episcopato* (Naples, 1977) 97-101. G. Ferraro relies on the interpretation of Numbers 11:16-17 by Philo of Alexandria, Origen, Augustine, Cyril of Alexandria, and Theodoret.

30. Ferraro, *Le preghiere di ordinazione* 109-115.

31. This New Testament type, which speaks of the companions of the Apostles, was enlarged by the 1989 revision to include a Christological dimension. Both our formulary and that of 1968 make no mention of Christ's priesthood and mission. This was considered by the revisors as something negative in as much as the presbyters' priestly function is not given a Christological foundation. Thus before mentioning the assistants of the Apostles, the 1989 formulary gives the following premise: *Novissime vero, Pater sancte, Filium tuum in mundum misisti, Apostolum et Pontificem confessionis nostrae Iesum.* The words *Apostolus et Pontifex* are found in Hebrews 3:1.

32. Apostolic Constitution *Pontificalis Romani*, editio typica altera (Vatican City, 1989) xi.

33. O. Casel, "Leitourgia-Munus," *Oriens Christianus* 3 (1932) 289; H. Frank, "Leitourgia-Munus," *Jahrbuch für Liturgiewissenschaft* 13 (1935) 181.

34. The Veronese formulary makes no reference to the office of deacons in the New Testament; see B. Kleinheyer, "La riforma degli Ordini sacri: Saggio storico liturgico sui nuovi riti," *Rivista Liturgica* 56 (1969) 8-24. The 1968 revisors added a new paragraph about the seven men whom the Apostles appointed to assist at table service (Acts 6:1-6). G. Ferraro discusses the background of this text, recalling three exegetical interpretations. The first holds that the seven men were not ordained deacons in the true sense of the word; the second goes to the other extreme and claims that the seven were ordained bishops; the third, the traditional, sees in this text the institution of the diaconate through prayer and hand laying by the Apostles; see *Le preghiere di ordinazione* 50-53.

35. *Missale Francorum*, ed. C. Molhberg (Rome, 1957) 7:21.

36. Ferraro, *Le preghiere di ordinazione* 63. (Münster, 1989) 26.

4

Liturgical Music and Its Early Cultural Setting

ONE OF THE GREAT ACHIEVEMENTS OF THE LITURGICAL MOVEMENT AND the conciliar reform is having the assembly sing the liturgy. In the last four hundred years there were remarkable efforts to involve the assembly through songs, even if most of the time these had nothing to do with the Order of Mass. There was singing during Mass, but the Mass was not sung. The liturgical notion of music is, strictly speaking, music that is joined to the liturgical text assigned to a particular moment in the celebration. Liturgical music means singing at the appointed time the assigned text: an antiphon or song, a formulary, a greeting and a response. One of the aims of liturgical music is to develop musical liturgy wherein the liturgical action is carried out in song, not merely accompanied by music. In this sense purely instrumental music, like a sonata for organ, would not pass today for liturgical music, although it may be used in liturgical celebrations to add solemnity or sometimes to fill a vacant "acoustic space." "Musical instruments whether accompanying the singing or played alone, can add a great deal to liturgical celebrations."[1]

Over the centuries the music used in the liturgy has been known under various names: ecclesiastical or church music, religious music, sacred music, and liturgical music.[2] Although each of these names has a particular history and usage, it is not possible at this point in time to give hard and fast definition to each. The truth is that today there is still fluidity in the use of these terms. Ecclesiastical or church music, a name which comes from ancient times, distinguished itself from the music used at secular gatherings. Today it denotes virtually any type of music used at congregational worship, whether liturgical or devotional. Thus Gregorian chant, the Lutheran hymns for worship like "A Mighty Fortress is Our God," and Catholic novena songs like "Immaculate Mother," all fall under the general category of church music. Religious music, on the other hand, refers to any type of music whose text is considered to have a religious theme, even if its rhythm is not traditionally used in church services, like jazz and rock. Religious music has a rather wide range: from rock music like "Jesus Christ Superstar," to African-American spirituals like "Where you there," to baroque music, like J.S. Bach's "Passion According to St. Matthew."

Sacred music is the official term used by recent Roman Church documents for the type of music composed for the celebration of the liturgy. The Instruction of 1958 is called *De Musica Sacra*. Chapter VI of Vatican II's Constitution on Liturgy carries the title "Sacred Music." In line with this, the 1967 Instruction on music is named *Musicam Sacram*. This particular Instruction explains that "music is 'sacred' insofar as it is composed for the celebration of divine worship and possesses integrity of form."[3] The definition is broad and embraces "Gregorian chant, the several styles of polyphony, both ancient and modern, sacred music for organ and for other permitted instruments, and the sacred, i.e., liturgical or religious, music of the people." Thus, sacred music is not necessarily tied to the liturgical text. It can be purely instrumental, provided it is recognized as something suited for worship. And it can be popular liturgical or religious music. Examples of popular liturgical music are songs approved by the conferences of bishops for use as entrance, offertory, and communion songs. Though more limited in scope than religious music, sacred music accommodates practically any form of church music.

Liturgical music is a more recent term and has enlisted a growing number of liturgists who prefer it to other terms. In his classic work cited above, J. Gelineau offers a penetrating insight into the nature and role of music in the liturgy.[4] His basic distinction between music *in* the liturgy and music *of* the liturgy clarifies what liturgical music is all about. Liturgical music is not any kind of music occurring during a liturgical celebration, regardless of whether or not it corresponds to the spirit of the liturgy or to the part of the celebration. One can think of such examples, which are not unheard of even today, as a novena song to Our Lady for communion (this is not in harmony with the spirit of the liturgy) or an offertory song for the entrance procession (this ignores the meaning of the entrance rite). Liturgical music is music whose lyric or text comes directly from the liturgical *ordo* or has been approved for liturgical use. E. Foley defines it as "that music which weds itself to the liturgical action, serves to reveal the full significance of the rite and, in turn, derives its full meaning from the liturgy."[5]

This definition shows the three components of liturgical music. First, it is woven into the liturgical rite and becomes an element of the celebration. The singing of the *Gloria* or the *Sanctus* at the prescribed time is part of the community's liturgical action. The offertory song while the gifts are brought to the presider is not merely for the sake of musical accompaniment; when performed, it becomes an element of the offertory rite, it becomes a liturgical action. Second, liturgical music has a symbolic nature and role: it reveals the meaning of the liturgical action. This means that its lyric corresponds to what goes on during the celebration and explains its deeper meaning. The text is basic to the notion of liturgical music. The Constitution on the Sacred Liturgy (art. 33) tells us that "although the liturgy is above all things the worship of the divine majesty, it likewise contains rich instruction for the faithful." Singing a liturgical text is an effective way of transmitting that "rich instruction" to the assembly. And third, liturgical music derives its full meaning from the liturgy. The purpose of liturgical music cannot be isolated from the purpose of the liturgy itself: it is composed and performed for the service of the liturgy. We may say that it has a ministerial role, outside of which it loses its meaning.

The aim of this chapter is to review the development of liturgical music in the early church before the eighth century, with special attention to the influence exerted upon it by culture as well as the prevailing theological thinking of the times.[6] For greater clarity of exposition the material is arranged chronologically rather than thematically.

LITURGICAL MUSIC IN THE FIRST CENTURY

Scholars advance the opinion that the music for the liturgy adopted by the church in the first century was borrowed principally from the synagogue and home. This type of music became the model for centuries to come. We may explain this by the first Christian community's closer association with the synagogal and domestic forms of worship than with the cult of the temple. The synagogue provided Christians with the liturgy of the word, whereas the eucharist was a sacred meal they celebrated at home. Word, sacrament, and home are the three chief elements of the early Christian worship. The temple in Jerusalem did not serve the church's forms of worship, since the temple was not the normal place for the proclamation of the word, nor was it the place for family meals. The first disciples continued to worship in the temple (Acts 3:1) and perhaps offered there the prescribed sacrifices (Acts 20:16). But their typical form of worship as a Christian community was synagogal (Acts 19:18) and domestic (Acts 2:46; 20:7-12). Even after the Nazarites, as Christians were then called, no longer attended the synagogal services, they continued to read the Jewish Scriptures at home gatherings. In short, the word and the eucharist, which constitute the nucleus of Christian worship, were musically influenced by the synagogue and the home. On the other hand, after the temple was destroyed in the year 70, the memory of the temple and its music was lost in the mist of time.

The temple music did not interest the young church probably because it did not possess the kind of organization and instruments the temple had. Even in the time of Jesus professional singers and instrumentalists rendered their services during temple celebrations. Instrumental music was part of temple ritual actions. The *shofar* or horns and trumpets, for example, announced the entrance of priests. Harps and lyres, on the other hand, were proper to levites. These stringed instruments were allied to the art of poetry, and thus were suited to accompany the psalms and other temple songs. They had a way of sustaining the lyric of the song and focusing attention to it. This is why, harps and lyres were regarded as properly liturgical instruments. 1 Chronicles 25:1-3 tells us that "for the liturgy, David and the senior army officers set apart the sons of Asaph, of

Heman, and of Jeduthun." These were "prophets" who accompanied themselves with lyre, harp, and cymbal. The Chronicler attributes prophetic characteristics to liturgical chant performed "to the sound of the lyre." Bells, tambourines, and cymbals were also used to accompany liturgical singing. But flutes, pipes, and oboes were considered lay instruments to be used at family or social affairs, especially marriages and funerals. Temple liturgical singing was performed by a trained choir which numbered at least twelve adult male singers.[7]

Psalm 150 names some of the instruments used in temple liturgical services: "Praise him with the sound of trumpet, praise him with lute and harp, praise him with timbrel and dance, praise him with strings and pipe, praise him with the clashing of cymbals."

The church of the third and fourth centuries, as we shall see, had little or no sympathy for musical instruments, because instruments were often associated with pagan worship or with immorality. The church of the first century, on the other hand, could not afford them; they would have been regarded as luxury items for a small group of believers gathered in a private house. The question of immorality or pagan worship would not have been raised, since musical instruments were part of the temple service. Nonetheless, we cannot categorically exclude the use of all musical instruments from domestic liturgies. It is probable that by and large the lyre or the harp was used to accompany songs. But there seems to be also a theological reason, possibly in the subconscious of the Christian community, why musical instruments did not form part of the liturgy. Was it the awareness that the Christian cult derived from the synagogal and domestic, rather than temple, tradition? We know that the synagogal liturgy definitely excluded the playing of musical instruments, except the horn to signal the feast.

The temple was staffed by professional instrumentalists and singers. The synagogue, on the other hand, made do with local talents and resources. Until the destruction of the temple in Jerusalem, when the dislocated professionals moved to the synagogues, the synagogal service, which centered on prayer and the word, had no place for musical instruments and choirs. Its chief activity revolved around the proclamation or reading of the word and the recitation of the *Shema* (see Dt 6:4-7, 9) and the

Amida or eighteen benedictions. A consideration of major significance to the history of liturgical music is how these elements of synagogal worship, namely reading and recitation of liturgical formularies, were rendered. Scholars tell us that in ancient times reading or public speaking and singing were not as clearly distinguishable as they are today. In other words, the scriptural reading and the blessings and prayers must have been proclaimed with some degree of melody. E. Foley explains that "the audible nature of all reading presumed rhythmic and melodic features that today would be more quickly classified as music rather than as speech. Public speaking, too, presumed a kind of chanting in cadence that fell someplace between modern categories of speech and song."[8]

This manner of reading and speaking in public is a musical genre known as "recitative" as opposed to "air." It is performed through cantillation or recitation of a text with musical tones or a set of melodic formulas. It can be described as a type of musical declamation in which both the structure and meaning of the text are respected, in which the purpose of the music is to be a vehicle of proclamation. Its reason for being is the lyric or text. As J. Gelineau has pointed out, the "recitative [unlike the "air"] is so bound up with words, that playing the melody without them would be meaningless. It is the text which gives to the melody the completion of its form; the melody alone cannot subsist without the words which give it existence."[9] This is the musical tradition which the early church inherited from the word-centered synagogal form of worship. It is the tradition preserved in the official Roman liturgy, where the presidential prayers, the eucharistic prayer with its various prefaces, the proclamation from Sacred Scripture and patristic literature, and the diaconal directions or intentions are cantillated.

The domestic liturgy of Judaism with its preference for music joined to a formulary also influenced the early church's liturgical music. The blessings chanted before meals, the psalms, and hymns were normal elements of Jewish home liturgies. Although we do not possess documents to prove that the psalms were used by Christians in their assemblies before the third century, Christological hymns patterned after Jewish models are found in the New Testament. Ephesians 1:4-14, Philippians 2:6-11, and Colossians 1:15-20 are examples of such hymns. One thing we should bear in mind is that the central position held in the synagogue and Jewish homes by the word of God and the liturgical formularies, or in short the word-centeredness of their celebrations, would in turn not have permitted florid musical arrangements to be used in Christian worship. Such arrangements would have been regarded as detracting from the primacy of the word or the liturgical text in the liturgy. The "recitative" would have been the typical musical genre employed by the emerging church of the first century. As far down as the time of St. Augustine this musical tradition was kept alive. J. Quasten informs us: "In the West it was primarily Augustine who was intent on not letting melodic beauty become the main concern in ecclesiastical singing. He permitted singing only for the sake of the text."[10]

LITURGICAL MUSIC FROM THE SECOND
TO THE FOURTH CENTURY

Till the fourth century liturgical music continued to develop in the context of the house church. It was a type of music suited to the setting of a domestic liturgy, of a "private" celebration within the confines of a *triclinium*. For this reason authors believe that the practice of cantillation continued to be the norm, especially for biblical readings and the prayers said by the presider of the assembly. It is likely that at this time the eucharistic prayer was delivered in a recitative tone, possibly patterned on the Jewish tradition of chanting the meal blessing. It seems that the distinction between public speaking and singing had not yet been established. Thus, the two principal elements of the liturgy, namely scriptural reading and the prayers by the presider, were performed according to the earlier tradition of music whose chief, perhaps only, purpose was to deliver or proclaim the word or the liturgical text.

Besides Scripture and prayer formularies, there were other elements of the domestic liturgy: psalms, nonbiblical songs, and hymns. As regards the psalms, there is no record before the end of the second century that psalms were used in Christian worship. Of course this does not indicate, contrary to some authors, that Christians did not recite psalms during worship. Silence is not a sufficient argument against the liturgical use of psalms in the early church. Rather, because of the church's strong synagogal tradition, which is probably the basis of St. Paul's admonition "to sing psalms, hymns, and spiritual canticles to God" (Col 3:16), we may suppose that from the very start psalms already formed part of Christian worship. Since the "great Hallel" or Psalms 112-117 was an element of the Passover meal, which was a domestic celebration, we can presume that at the Passover season Christians would have revived this Jewish tradition. At any rate, the chanting of psalms is reported by the apocryphal *Acts of Paul* 7,10, written toward the year 190: "Each shared in the bread, and they feasted . . . to the sound of David's psalms and hymns." Tertullian in his work *On the Soul* informs us that in Christian assemblies "the Scriptures are read and psalms are sung, allocutions are delivered and prayers offered."[11] It is interesting to note that this liturgy was held *in ecclesia inter dominica sollemnia*, which can only mean the Sunday eucharist. Its *ordo* consisted of scriptural reading, followed by the chanting of psalms, the homily, and prayers, or in short of what is known today as the liturgy of the word. The position of the psalms between the readings and the homily seems to witness to the early tradition of the responsorial psalm at Mass.[12]

Nonbiblical psalms, known to scholars as *psalmi idiotici*, began to appear at this time. These were compositions by Christians in the style of the psalms, and hence could be sung like psalms. The earliest examples of such are the *Odes of Solomon*, written in the second century. Part of Ode 27 reads: "I extended my hands and hallowed my Lord, For the expansion of my hands is his sign. And my extension is the upright cross. Hallelujah."[13] We may say that nonbiblical psalms answered the Christian need to sing "psalms" that are directly and explicitly Christian. Although we read in Luke 24:44 that everything written in the psalms about Christ had to be fulfilled, it requires some mental process, which is not always accessible to all, to recognize Christ in them. The later tradition of concluding the psalms with the trinitarian doxology supports the Christian interpretation of the Jewish psalms.

Through nonbiblical psalms the early church sang to the Lord in words that proclaim directly his person and mystery. We may imagine that in Christian assemblies the singing of nonbiblical psalms was a rather normal occurrence. It offered an opportunity to individuals to proclaim in song their faith and experience of Christ, comparable to the modern personal witnessing of faith in charismatic gatherings. In his *Apologeticum* Tertullian mentions the practice of singing privately composed psalms: "After the ritual handwashing and the bringing in of the lights, each one is invited to stand and sing to God as one is able: either something from the holy scriptures or of one's own making."[14] With typical irony Tertullian adds, in answer to the pagan accusation of drunkenness in Christian assemblies, "hereby we are able to prove how much one has drunk!" It was indeed an era of spontaneity and improvisation, and we may surmise that the manner of singing these songs depended to a large extent on the talent of the individual. Tertullian's words "as one is able" (*proprio ingenio*), which Hippolytus also applies to the bishop when he speaks of the eucharistic prayer, seem to confirm this. It is important to remember that the liturgy at that time was celebrated in a domestic setting, where one would expect a measure of spontaneity.

Hymns also formed part of the early church's worship, or in the words of J. Gelineau, they have always been "on the threshold of liturgy."[15] Unlike psalms, hymns are metrical poems divided into stanzas of at least two lines. Each stanza has the same meter, number of syllables, scheme of word accent, and number of verse lines. This trait allows for the singing of each stanza in the same way as the first. When such a trait is not observed by the composer, as in the case of the *Gloria* and *Te Deum*, singing suffers because of adjustments made on notation. On the other hand, the singing of the psalms, which are not metered like the hymns, requires modification of the music, however slightly, in order to accommodate the varying meter, number of syllables, and word accents. In the situation of the domestic church it would appear that hymns were sung by the assembly, rather than by a choir of singers. The letter of Pliny the Younger to Emperor Trajan in the year 112 reports that the assembled Christians sang hymns alternately among themselves, that is, the assembly must have been divided into two groups. Pliny writes: "They were accustomed to meet on a fixed day before dawn and sing alternately among themselves a hymn to Christ as to a god."[16]

A famous hymn to Christ, in Greek, dating from the early third century was composed by Clement of Alexandria whom authors suspect to have been influenced by second-century Gnostic hymns. In translation it reads: "King of saints, almighty Word of the Father, highest Lord, Wisdom's head and chief, assuagement of all grief; Lord of all time and space: Jesus, Savior of our race."[17] The only example of a musically annotated hymn dating from the third century was discovered in a papyrus from Oxyrhyncos in Egypt. Musicologists have been able to transcribe its melody, which is definitely not of the "recitative" genre, but is closer to what is called "air." Composed in Greek, the fragment in translation reads: ". . . neither the stars, sources of light, nor the springs whence flow the raging torrents are silent! While we sing the praises of Father, Son, and Holy Spirit, let all the powers cry out: Amen, Amen! Power and glory to the sole giver of all good things: Amen, Amen!"[18] Unlike the nonbiblical psalms which could be composed on the spur of the moment or at the inspiration of the singer, hymns had established lyrics and music which rendered them easily accessible to the assembly.

During this period we notice the absence of reference to special singers, psalmists, or cantors. The reader and the presider, of course, chanted or cantillated their parts, but the assembly sang the rest, especially the psalms and hymns. Before the fourth century the shape of the liturgy was still very much a domestic affair in which there was as yet no need for a trained or professional choir. Furthermore, it is useful to remember that the entire liturgy was musical. The readings and prayers were cantillated, and the psalms, both biblical and nonbiblical, as well as the hymns were sung. No part of the liturgy would have been spoken. For us who have grown used to the idea of *Missa lecta*, alas even on Sunday, a musical liturgy might appear as curious as the rhythmic swaying, mistakenly called dancing, at processions in African churches. When one approached the altar in procession, one did not simply walk: one swayed in rhythmic movement. Similarly, when one proclaimed the word, one did not simply speak: one cantillated the text. Such was the musical setting in which the liturgy of the church began to evolve from the second to the fourth century.

Obviously this musical tradition is foreign to many cultures. Some find the chanted greeting "The Lord be with you" as amusing as would be a chanted "good morning." Yet we should probably be wary of easy cultural analogies. The liturgy is a ritual action that has developed a cultural pattern distinctly its own. Chanting greetings and prayers, or even biblical readings, should not surpise us anymore than the required singing of "happy birthday to you." No one would think of merely reciting the lyrics of this song.

Which instruments did the early church use for liturgical services? J. Gelineau writes: "We cannot say definitely that during the patristic era Christians never made use of certain instruments, such as the lyre, to accompany their liturgical singing. Certain passing allusions or repeated prohibitions even lead to the conclusion that this was a well-established practice."[19] Yet we come across strongly worded prohibitions against using in the liturgy certain musical instruments, like the flute and the music pipe or *aulos*. Clement of Alexandria, who died in the year 215, condemns in his *The Pedagogue* the use of trumpets, *aulos*, lyre, horn, and cymbals. "These instruments," he writes, "should be excluded from the sober repast [of Christians]; they are more fitted to charm animals than people, or people who are deprived of their reason." Clement goes on to interpret the musical instruments mentioned in Psalm 150 in a purely allegorical sense. In actual practice they are of no use except for inciting to war, stimulating the passions, inflaming lust, or arousing anger. And he concludes by saying that "we make use only of a single, peaceful instrument, the *Logos*, by which we honor God."[20] Sometime at the beginning of the fifth century the Syrian Pseudo-Justin wrote: "Singing is not a childish matter, but singing to the accompaniment of inanimate instruments, dancing, and shaking rattles is. Hence, in churches the use of instruments and other childish things have been excluded from songs, though singing is retained."[21]

As far down as the fourth century we meet a certain reticence in the use of musical instruments. John Chrysostom in his homilies on Psalm 149 explains that God permitted the Jewish people to use musical instruments "out of regard for the weakness of their spirit, and because they had hardly emerged as yet from the cult of idols."[22] On the other hand, Augustine of Hippo makes an allegorical interpretation of the instruments in Psalm 150 in his treatise on the same psalm: "It is you who are the trumpet, the psaltery, the harp, the tympanum, the chorus of dancers, the strings, organ and cymbals of jubilation, well sounding because concordant. It is you who are all these. There is no allusion here to anything despicable or ephemeral, or which would be mere amusement."[23]

Thus, whereas the first-century church did not use musical instruments for temple services because of its synagogal tradition, the church from the second to the fourth century excluded musical instruments like flutes and castanets from the liturgy because of their association with the worship of idols, licentious meals, and the theatre and dances of lascivious character. B. Cole makes the following reminder: "It has to be kept in mind that those Fathers who were negative about the music of their period were not making aesthetic judgments about pure music as we know it, a recent art by historical standards. Rather, most of these Fathers condemned the drunkenness and lewd dances which in many instances were associated with it."[24] In fact, the various patristic references to musical instruments until the fifth century ran the gamut of all the possible attitudes: from approval, to reticence, to an allegorical acceptance, and to condemnation. It was only in the Middle Ages that the church in the west introduced organs, harps, guitars, flutes, bagpipes, cornets, and other instruments to accompany the voices in polyphony or religious processions.

LITURGICAL MUSIC FROM THE FIFTH TO THE EIGHTH CENTURY

"Moving worship from the house church to the basilica meant not only a change in the architectural space but also in the acoustic space."[25] Unlike the *domus ecclesiae*, the basilica, which the Christians of the Constantinian era adopted for their public worship, was an imperial hall, one that encouraged grand, almost theatrical, celebrations. If we consider that the bishop of Rome adopted the imperial insignia and was treated according to the ceremonials of the imperial court, we can understand the profound influence of the basilica on liturgical music. Just as the emperor was greeted by a choir when he entered the basilica, so was the bishop of Rome. The entrance song then had a quite different purpose from what it has today, except at some pontifical Masses where the entrance song *Ecce sacerdos magnus* is in fact a greeting addressed to the presiding bishop. In contrast to the simple musical tradition of the house church, choirs had to be trained for the specialized ministry of singing. It was during the pontificate of Sergius I (687-701) that there appeared in Rome what later came to be known as the *schola cantorum*. These singers were clerics who were trained from infancy to a very high technical standard of chant-singing. To them we owe the composition of the Roman chant which later developed into the so-called Gregorian chant.

A development which has had repercussion on the role of women in church choirs is the clericalization of the *schola cantorum*. J. Quasten tells us that "as the boy choir superseded the cantor, so individual boys from the choir gradually took the place of the lector, whose office was often connected with that of the cantor."[26] He mentions, among other regulations, the decretal of Pope Siricius, who died in 398, requiring those who wished to dedicate themselves to the service of the church from childhood to begin as lectors. The linking of the *schola cantorum* to the office of lector clericalized the former. Hence a boy lector, chosen from the boy choir, in effect became a cleric. This was probably the background for the prohibition by the Synods of Auxerre in the years 561-604 against admitting laymen and women into the *schola cantorum*. The ministry of singing in choir during liturgical functions became a clerical reserve to which women had no access.

J. Quasten notes that during the first two centuries women took part in liturgical singing as members of the assembly. In the third century heretics began to establish choirs of women separated from the rest of the assembly. Among heretics, women enjoyed the exalted ranks of prophets, lectors, deacons, and singers. Was this the reason why a century later some of the Church Fathers, among them St. Cyril of Jerusalem, reacted against women's choirs and sometimes also against women's participation in congregational singing? But this negative attitude was not universal. St. Ambrose defended their participation by affirming that singing the psalms was fitting for every age and for both sexes. On the other hand, St. Ephrem founded choirs of virgins and taught them to sing hymns and responses to counteract the heretical choirs of women. According to J. Quasten, the exclusion of women from singing as choir and finally from singing as members of the assembly was motivated by the church's struggle against heresies and the liturgical practices of heretics like the establishment of women's choir. His thesis, however, does not necessarily exclude the factor of clericalization. At any rate, the question cannot be viewed from the angle of culture but of church discipline.

Whereas the liturgy of the house church did not require trained musicians, the imperial liturgy encouraged professionalism in music. *Roman Ordo* I, which describes a papal Mass in the seventh century, speaks of a *schola* led by a *prior scholae* or head cantor. It was the *schola*, and it would seem the *schola* alone, that rendered the entrance, offertory, and communion songs.[27] It is not clear from this *Ordo* whether the assembly sang anything at all, though we have no reason to believe that the responses to the greetings and the psalms, and perhaps the *Gloria* and the *Sanctus*, were not chanted congregationally. The point is that the ambience of the basilica necessitated the composition of a more elaborate type of liturgical music at the expense of popular participation.

Yet notwithstanding the imperial character of the liturgy at this period, liturgical music retained the traditional "recitative" form or cantillation in the proclamation of biblical texts and the presidential orations. And this is significant, because it shows that the original core, namely the centrality of the word, was preserved in the process of change in "acoustic space."

It was toward the sixth century when the Roman Church began to develop its liturgical chant and continued to do so until the thirteenth century. In the middle of the ninth century this ancient Roman chant was ascribed to Gregory the Great who died in the year 604, and thus it came to be known as Gregorian chant. According to J. Gelineau, the original stratum of the Roman chant "is made up of the recitatives of readings and prayers, the verses of psalms, the acclamations and the dialogues, and some of the most ancient of the hymns."[28] This recitative quality of the original Roman chant, which exalts the lyrics rather than the melody, is what defines this music as liturgical. Thus, he affirms that "beyond all doubt the perfect wedding of text to music is one of the most remarkable characteristics of Gregorian chant; it is this quality which explains why Gregorian chant is liturgical par excellence and why it remains, in this respect, the model for all music pertaining to a rite."[29]

As examples, J. Gelineau mentions the Roman tones for the gospel reading, the prefaces, the opening prayers, *Gloria XV* and *Sanctus XVIII* in the Roman collection *Liber Usualis*, and the *Te Deum*. Their music, he explains, is allied with the Jewish cantillations, and can claim to be rooted in the early tradition of liturgical music. It is a syllabic type of music, which means that normally there would only be one or at most two notes per syllable. This type of chant was especially suited for congregational singing.

What is known today as the corpus of Gregorian chant is a repertoire of compositions from every epoch in every musical genre and style. In reality pieces continue to be composed, in order to set new Latin liturgical formularies to music. Understandably these recent compositions imitate the older ones or are the result of fitting existing Gregorian melodies to new texts. For example, the antiphons for lauds and vespers of Christ the King use the melody for the first vespers of Christmas.

The rise of professional singers during the Constantinian era led to the evolution of the ancient system of cantillation to complex ornamentation and melodic developments. Such musical genre required professional soloists or choirs with advanced vocal techniques. They excluded the participation of the assembly. Examples of these in the Gregorian corpus are the neumatic pieces, like several introits and communion antiphons, and the melismatic graduals that are prolix in musical ornamentation. In these instances the interest is no longer in the text but in the melody. Thus liturgical music evolved from the "recitative" to the "air," in which the melody and the rhythm become autonomous entities, that is, independent from the text. Even in our day there are liturgical composers whose immediate concern is the melody rather than the liturgical text. In the process the text or the formulary must adjust itself to the preconceived melody, to the point of having parts of the text repeated or, alas, at times even mutilated.

Another trait of this period is the flowering of hymnody. We know that hymns were an ancient element of Christian worship. According to A. Adam, "from the fourth century on, *hymns,* which in early Christianity usually had quite simple texts and melodies, showed advances in textual and musical quality."[30] St. Ambrose of Milan is regarded as the father of western hymnody, and it is possible that his hymns were sung to well-known secular tunes of the time, as Martin Luther had some of his centuries later. Some hymns were presumably sung during the eucharistic liturgy, and more so in the divine office from the time of St. Benedict of Nursia in the sixth century. However, in the Roman tradition hymns have not been constitutive elements of the eucharistic celebration and thus they tended to remain at the periphery of the liturgical action. The variable songs for the entrance, offertory, and communion rites are drawn from psalms, though their antiphons may be nonbiblical compositions.

After the Council of Trent there were efforts to engage the faithful during Mass, where the use of Latin had reduced the assembly to mere spectators. In 1605 the *Cantuale of Mainz* was produced to allow the congregation to sing popular hymns at the time of the gradual, after the narration of the institution, in place of *Agnus Dei*, and at communion. At a time when the liturgy of the Roman Mass had already acquired its definitive texts and formularies, which did not include hymns, such a practice, though pastorally laudable, did not make the people sing the liturgy; all it did was to make them sing during the liturgy. Today, however, perhaps under Lutheran influence, it is quite common among Catholics to sing hymns in place of psalms as entrance, offertory, and communion songs. The chief consideration here is active participation.

Liturgical hymnody did not always and everywhere receive the sympathy of church authorities. The Roman divine office, in fact, did not have hymns. It was St. Benedict who introduced Ambrosian hymns into the monastic *opus Dei*, whence they passed over to the Roman office. Hymns were popular because the assembly found their melody simple and engaging. No amount of prohibition could put a stop to the practice of singing hymns during public worship. In 563 the first Council of Braga, canon 12, decreed that except for the psalms or other biblical passages from the Old and New Testaments, no poetic compositions, that is, hymns, may be sung in liturgical gatherings. The preoccupation here was, of course, to hold at bay heretical doctrines which could easily creep into such poetic compositions.

But such a measure did not stifle the production of liturgical hymns. From the fourth century there was a demand for hymns. A. Adam estimates that "about 35,000 hymns in all were composed" after the fourth century.[31]

The flowering of hymnody was symptomatic of the gradual decline of active participation of the faithful in the liturgy, particularly the eucharist. Singing hymns meant *singing during Mass*, rather than *singing the Mass*. The rise of professional singers at first confined the role of the assembly to the recitative parts of the liturgy. But even these began to be abandoned in later centuries, in favor of the more ornate and talent-demanding genre called melismatic music. Thus the assembly had to content itself with hymns, which were not necessarily constitutive of the liturgy of the Roman Mass. Today, however, hymns are no longer extraneous to the Roman Mass: they are often sung as processional songs. This is surely a most welcome development, even if it requires a great effort on the part of local churches to be creative, while being attentive to the nature of the liturgy as well as the musical tradition and lyrical genius of each people. Apropos the local churches with native musical tradition distinct from the western, J. Gelineau writes: "It is particularly desirable that in mission countries native compositions should be encouraged rather than the imported tunes of European hymns, for they can suit the musical idiom of the country and the poetry which belongs to the language concerned."[32]

* * * * * * * *

In Jewish as well as other ancient cultures proclamation and public speaking, because of their solemn character, were not merely read or spoken. They were cantillated. This was the practice in the synagogues from which Christian worship inherited it. It consisted of reciting a text with musical tones or with a set of melodic formula. For the early Christians, whose liturgy centered on the word of God and prayer formularies, cantillation was the best available form of music, because cantillation transmitted more effectively the message of the text. As a musical genre, it highlights the words and enhances their meaning. The proliferation of musical notes, on the other hand, has the tendency to obscure the text, while calling attention to the melody.

Early Christian music stressed the primacy of the lyrics or text and placed itself at the service of the word. It shared in the church's ministry of preaching the word.

From the beginning, the liturgy did not consist only of biblical readings and prayer formularies. Psalms, which were sung in synagogues and homes, must have made their way into the homes and gatherings of Christians. And we can presume that the first converts continued to sing them in the way they were sung in synagogues and domestic religious celebrations. As early as the third century, nonbiblical songs—composed in the manner of psalms—became a popular element of Christian worship. Through them any individual could witness in song to the mystery of Christ and to one's faith-experience. From the earliest times hymns also formed part of Christian gatherings, as they formed part of the Jewish worship. Matthew 26:30 tells us that after the Last Supper Jesus and his disciples sang a hymn before they went out to the Mount of Olives. Hymnody was a normal element of people's musical as well as lyrical culture. When Pliny the Younger reported that Christians sang hymns to Christ as to a god, he implied that they were doing what the pagans would normally do during their worship, that is, sing hymns. There was no reason to arrest them for this.

Yet the *psalmi idiotici* and hymns were not always looked upon with sympathy, because their lyrics did not originate in Scripture. Was it perhaps a matter of prudence in the face of possible incursions of heresy through private authorship? What could be safer, doctrinally, than the word of God? At any rate, the church's reticence about and prohibition against using nonbiblical texts did not discourage the proliferation of hymns for the liturgy. Hymnody is a strong element of people's musical culture. When the greater portion of the eucharistic liturgy was turned over to the clergy and the professional musicians as their exclusive domain, the assembly had to content itself with singing hymns. Often hymns did not reflect the meaning of the liturgical rite. Nevertheless, it is in hymns where we are able to perceive most clearly the role of culture in the development of liturgical music, since hymns embody the people's poetic spirit and lyrical talent.

The transition from the *domus ecclesiae* to the Constantinian basilica affected liturgical music, as it did the liturgical rite, in a dramatic and lasting way. Unlike the domestic type of celebration, the solemn liturgy in the splendor of the spacious imperial hall required professional singers and trained choir. To match such solemnity, splendor, and artistic quality, liturgical music began to be ornamented with neums and melisma, which rendered them inaccessible to the majority of the assembly. It did not take the church very long to abandon the "recitative," that musical tradition which is so congenial to the word-centered liturgy of the church and to active participation.

But the present is built on the past. The development of liturgical music over the past centuries need not be viewed with regret. It seems historically unsound to consider only the early beginnings and ignore the rest. Returning exclusively to the "recitative" genre might not be the only answer to the question of singing the Mass instead of singing during Mass, of the primacy of the word, or of active participation. Musical culture has evolved, and it is not rare to find people who concentrate on the lyrics of an aria in an opera, cantata, or oratorio. What reason is there to say that polyphony is not suited for the liturgy? Why should not an assembly sing in voices? Why should we be content with mediocre congregational singing and equally mediocre, if not absolutely trite, musical compositions? There seems to be no reason why a trained choir should not, on occasion, render greater solemnity to the liturgy by singing certain parts of the Mass, for example, the entrance, offertory, and communion songs. In our contemporary world trained choirs and excellence in musical performance are highly prized; they are valued components of cultural life. Surely the liturgy should not be deprived of the beauty and nobility of contemporary culture. In our preoccupation to enhance the word and foster active participation through song, have we not perhaps forgotten that musical art is part of our liturgical tradition?

Notes

1. Sacred Congregation of Rites, Instruction *Musicam Sacram*, *Notitiae* 3 (1967) no. 62; English translation in *Documents on the Liturgy*, henceforth DOL (Collegeville, 1982) 1305.

2. J. Gelineau, *Voices and Instruments in Christian Worship* (Collegeville, 1964) 59-65.

3. Instruction *Musicam Sacram*, no. 4; DOL 1294.

4. Gelineau, *Voices and Instruments* 59-65.

5. E. Foley, "Liturgical Music," *The New Dictionary of Sacramental Worship* (Collegeville, 1990) 855.

6. For historical material I depend on the following authors (in alphabetical order): B. Cole, *Music and Morals* (New York, 1993); E. Foley, "Liturgical Music," *The New Dictionary of Sacramental Worship* (Collegeville, 1990) 854-870; E. Foley, *From Age to Age: How Christians Celebrated the Eucharist* (Chicago, 1991); E. Foley, *Foundations of Christian Music: The Music of Pre-Constantinian Christianity* (Nottingham, 1991); E. McKenna, "Styles of Liturgical Music," *The New Dictionary of Sacramental Worship* (Collegeville, 1990) 870-881; J. McKinnon, *Music in Early Christian Literature* (Cambridge, 1987); J. Quasten, *Music and Worship in Pagan and Christian Antiquity* (Washington, D.C., 1983).

7. Gelineau, *Voices and Instruments* 148-152.

8. Foley, *From Age to Age* 9.

9. Gelineau, *Voices and Instruments* 113.

10. Quasten, *Music and Worship* 93.

11. *De Anima*, 9,4, Corpus Christianorum, vol. 2:2 (1954) 792.

12. A. Verheul, "Le psaume responsorial dans la liturgie eucharistique," *Questions liturgiques* 73:4 (1992) 232-252.

13. See the English translation in Foley, *From Age to Age* 31.

14. *Apologeticum* 39,18, Corpus Christianorum, vol. 2:1 (1954) 153.

15. Gelineau, *Words and Instruments* 183-191.

16. English text in R. Cabié, *History of the Mass* (Washington, D.C., 1992) 22.

17. English text in E. Foley, *From Age to Age* 32.

18. The text and musical notation of this hymn are reproduced by J. Gelineau, *Voices and Instruments* 55.

19. Ibid. 150; see J. Quasten, *Music and Worship* 72-75.

20. *The Pedagogue* II,4, Sources chrétiennes, vol. 108 (1965) 93.

21. *Questions Addressed to the Orthodox* 107, PG 6:1353-1355.

22. *Homily on Psalm 149*, PG 55:494.

23. *Enarratio in Ps. 150*, PL 37:1965-1966.

24. Cole, *Music and Morals* 51.

25. Foley, *From Age to Age* 49.

26. Quasten, *Music and Worship* 90.

27. *Les Ordines Romani du haut moyen âge*, vol. 2, ed. M. Andrieu (Louvain, 1960) no. 60, p. 83; no. 85, p. 95; no. 112, p.107.

28. Gelineau, *Voices and Instruments* 195.

29. Ibid. 118.

30. A. Adam, *Foundations of Liturgy: An Introduction to Its History and Practice* (Collegeville, 1992) 82.

31. Ibid. 82.

32. Gelineau, *Voices and Instruments* 205.

5

Tradition and Progress: The Order of Mass Revisited

WHEN POPE PAUL VI PROMULGATED ON 3 APRIL 1969 THE TYPICAL edition of the Roman Missal (also called the Missal of Vatican II), he remarked, as if to forestall criticism on the part of people who wanted to retain the Missal of Pius V (also called the Tridentine Missal): "No one should think that this revision of the Roman Missal has come out of nowhere."[1] He pointed out that the discovery and publication of the ancient Christian sources and the progress in liturgical studies especially in our century have contributed immensely to the work of updating the Roman Missal published by Pope Pius V in 1570.

Vatican II decided that "the Order of Mass is to be revised in a way that will bring out more clearly the intrinsic nature and purpose of its several parts, as also the connection between them, and will more readily achieve the devout, active participation of the faithful."[2] The revision willed by the Council has three components. First, the various parts of the Mass should be neatly and semiotically defined. What, for example, is an entrance rite? What is its purpose, what are its elements, how does it begin, and when does it end? The same questions can be asked regarding the other parts of the Mass. Second, since the *ordo* is a cohesive whole, the relationship between its various parts should be evident to all. How does the liturgy of the word relate to the liturgy of the eucharist? What is the connection between the three scriptural readings, between the psalm and the first reading, or between the readings and the homily? Third, the revision should aim toward the devout and active participation of the assembly, for "in the reform and promotion of the liturgy, this full and active participation by all the people is the aim to be considered before all else" (SC 14). How, for example, can the assembly participate in the eucharistic prayer, that central prayer of the entire eucharist which Justin Martyr, a lay person in the congregation, referred to already in the second century as a "long prayer"?

LITURGICAL TRADITIONS IN THE MISSAL OF PAUL VI

How was the question of revision approached after the Council? The answer is, in the light of a tradition that the liturgical movement prior to Vatican II had advanced as the most suitable for intelligent and active participation. We refer to the Roman classical tradition dating from the fifth century and marked by textual and ritual simplicity, sobriety, and practical sense. Revision in this light meant streamlining the rite of the Mass considerably. Gone, for example, are the multiple opening prayers, the many signs of the cross during the Canon, and the repeated recitation of formularies of self-deprecation to which liturgists have attached the name "apologies." Likewise, those "elements that, with the passage of time, came to be duplicated or were added with but little advantage" were discarded. Examples of these are the repetitious prayers to accompany the preparation of bread and wine on the altar, the breaking of the consecrated bread, and the communion of the faithful. Finally, other parts of the Mass that "have suffered injury through accident of history are to be restored to the vigor they had in the tradition of the ancient Fathers." Examples of such elements are the homily and the general intercessions which disappeared from the Roman Mass in the early part of the Middle Ages. The seventh-century Gregorian Sacramentary, which contains an Order of Mass, mentions neither the homily nor the general intercessions. And there is no indication that these are implied or taken for granted by the text.[3]

But according to Pope Paul VI, "the chief innovation in the reform [of the Roman Missal] concerns the eucharistic prayer." The innovation is twofold. The pope proudly notes that in the new missal the eucharistic prayer has been enriched with a greater number of prefaces, especially for Sundays and ferial days. The second innovation is quite revolutionary. Contrary to the ancient Roman tradition of a single eucharistic prayer (until Vatican II the Roman rite used exclusively the fourth-century Roman Canon), three new eucharistic prayers have been added.[4] But the list of the outstanding innovations in the new missal would not be complete without mentioning the new Lectionary for the Mass. This book was designed to contain "a more representative portion of the holy Scripture to be read to the people over the course of a prescribed number of years."[5] For the first time in known history, approximately ninety percent of the holy Scripture has been included in the lectionary.

Those unfamiliar with the Tridentine Missal or Missal of Pius V might not readily appreciate the radical character of the innovations introduced by Paul VI. A few questions can perhaps help these people realize the extent of the innovations. As presiding priest, what sense will you make of reciting seven rather lengthy prayers as you prepare the eucharistic gifts on the altar? What meaning will you give to the practice of concluding the Mass with the reading of the Prologue to the Gospel of St. John? As member of the assembly, how will you react to the celebration of a Mass where the eucharistic prayer is enveloped in silence, where you are given holy communion with formularies for the communion of the sick, and where your presence is as good as ignored? As the General Instruction of the Roman Missal assures us, "when the more profound elements of the tradition [of the Fathers] are considered, it becomes clear how remarkably and harmoniously this new Roman Missal improves on the older one."[6] Obviously those who regard the Mass as pure devotion wrapped in mystery and in the "cloud of unknowing" or have little sympathy for intelligent and active participation will hardly agree with the above statement. Alas, romanticism deprived of historical and pastoral foundation has time and again behaved like a terrier snapping at the heels of conciliar reform.

The Missal of Paul VI did not come out of nowhere. First, it is technically a revision of the fourth-century-old Missal of Pius V. Some have had the audacity to consider the Missal of Pius V the touchstone of liturgical evolution. In reality, except for slight changes, it was nothing more than a repeat of the *Editio Princeps*, the first printed edition of 1474. Surely given the grave concern of the Roman Church over the Protestant liturgical innovations, the publication of the Tridentine Missal in 1570 was the best thing that happened to a church whose liturgical tradition was being disputed or simply ignored. But this did not make the missal the touchstone of many centuries of liturgical tradition. The *Editio Princeps* in turn was a faithful copy of the missal used in the time of Pope Innocent III who died in 1216.[7] On the other hand, the Missal of Paul VI differs immensely from its predecessor. One may doubt very much that Pope Pius V would be able to recognize the original text in the revised missal. The work of revision has been so thorough, that the Missal of Paul VI can, for practical purposes, be considered a new creation.

Yet Pope Paul VI would probably not want us to consider his missal a new creation. It is, at least technically, a revision of its predecessor. After all, revision was the type of work the Second Vatican Council had in mind when it approved article 50 of the Constitution on the Sacred Liturgy. By calling for revision rather than a new creation, the Council wanted to ensure that liturgical tradition would be preserved in the process of change. The question, however, is which liturgical tradition? We know that each of several liturgical sources we possess (let us simply call them liturgical books or documents) owns and projects a particular tradition. We are able to speak of an early patristic tradition from the second to the fourth century, of a classical Roman tradition from the fourth to the eighth century, and of a medieval tradition of which the Missal of Pius V is an eminent example.

The long and short of it is that we cannot confine our understanding of liturgical tradition to one tradition. There are several traditions because there is a variety of sources used by churches both in the east and the west. Indeed in the thinking of Pope Pius V an unchallenged practice of 200 years becomes a liturgical tradition. But we are not obliged to believe that the different traditions agree with each other on all matters, including important ones. The consecratory nature of the eucharistic epiclesis, which is tenaciously upheld by eastern churches, does not resonate with equal force in the Roman tradition. Ambrose of Milan attributed the effect of consecration to the *verba Christi*, the eucharistic words of Jesus repeated during the Canon.[8] The practice in the early tradition of giving the homily disappeared in the liturgy of the early Middle Ages or else was replaced in the thirteenth century by the dogmatic and moralistic sermons of mendicant preachers. Lastly, the sobriety and noble simplicity of the Roman classical tradition gave way to the dramatic and sensuous Franco-Germanic rituals.

Which tradition is represented in the revised Missal of Paul VI? The option was made by the Council itself, thanks to the liturgical scholars who had a special predilection for the traditions of the classical period and the patristic age. The Constitution on the Sacred Liturgy (art. 50) is very explicit on the kind of tradition the Council wanted: "The rites are to be simplified, due care being taken to preserve their substance; elements that, with the passage of time, came to be duplicated or were added but with little advantage are now to be discarded; other elements that have suffered injury through accident of history are now, as may seem useful or necessary, to be restored to the vigor they had in the traditions of the Fathers." Rites are to be simplified, duplications should be discarded, and useful or necessary elements should be restored in accord with patristic tradition. With these words the Council expressed its choice in favor of the classical shape of the Roman liturgy. The overriding consideration was, of course, not an archeological reconstruction of the past. In the thinking of those who framed the Constitution, a return to the classical Roman tradition could bring out more clearly the meaning and purpose of the eucharistic celebration and at the same time enhance devout and active participation of the faithful. They felt that the medieval form of the Mass, with its gross omissions and useless repetitions, often obscured the meaning of the rite.

What is meant by "tradition of the Fathers"? According to the General Instruction of the Roman Missal the "tradition of the Fathers" dates back to "the first centuries before the formation of the Eastern and Western rites" and includes "the Church's entire past and all the ways in which its single faith has been expressed in the quite diverse human and social forms prevailing in Semitic, Greek, and Latin cultures."[9] This is a rather broad definition of the liturgical tradition of the Fathers. In fact, it embraces the entire gamut of past practices from the Jewish to the Greco-Roman era. It is in the light of such tradition that the General Instruction regards the Missal of Paul VI as "a witness to unbroken tradition." The implication is that the postconciliar missal is not bound to a single tradition, even if it leans heavily on earlier and the classical Roman traditions. In this sense the revised missal represents what we may rightly regard as a compendium of select traditions found in the church. We are dealing here not with a single tradition but with several and quite distinct traditions. The parameter is wide. For example, the entrance rite alone has classical as well as Franco-Germanic elements.

To be honest about it, we can dare say that Pope Gregory the Great who died in the year 604 would probably be more at home with the Missal of Paul VI than would the popes from Pius V to John XXIII. The reason is that the new missal is much closer to the classical Roman form, known to Pope Gregory, than to its medieval predecessor.

STEPS FORWARD IN LITURGICAL TRADITION

In praise of the revised Missal of Paul VI, the General Instruction makes this affirmation: "As it bears witness to the Roman Church's rule of prayer (*lex orandi*) and guards the deposit of faith handed down by the later councils, the new Roman Missal marks a major step forward in liturgical tradition."[10] According to the Instruction the work of revising the missal has brought about a progress in liturgical tradition. Its thinking is clear: revision is not a departure from tradition; rather it is built on tradition and improves it. It cannot depart from the church's tradition which expresses the rule of prayer and the deposit of faith. However, tradition should move forward; it should be dynamic and progressive. We exert effort to discover our traditions, not so that we may enshrine and conserve them unaltered in liturgical books, but so that we may use them as means of advancement. Liturgical tradition is a living tradition: it is something contemporary, yet rooted in the past. This is why progress without tradition is like building on sand. Archeology and history are, in this sense, two basic components of liturgical progress.[11]

What are the implications of progress in liturgical tradition? What are the consequences of revising the missal on the basis of sources that date back to the fifth century and the Middle Ages? It would be quite tedious to try to discuss here the implications and consequences for each part of the missal. A couple of examples should sufficiently elucidate the question and, it is hoped, contribute to further considerations on other major steps forward in liturgical tradition.[12]

An area we may consider here concerns the prayer formularies of the missal. The collects, also called opening prayers (though in reality they conclude the entrance rite), the prayers over the gifts, and the prayers after communion in the present missal are taken in great number from ancient Roman sources.[13] Several of these prayers were composed and compiled between the fifth and the ninth century. Written in rhetorical Latin and with remarkable sobriety in the use of imagery, they tend to address the intellect and forget the heart. They employ a type of language and imagery that was typical of the classical period of the Roman liturgy: sober, direct, and simple, or in other words, lacking human elements that can rouse ordinary people to excitement.

The task of determining the source for each formulary in the new missal is simple enough. For translators the task is also a cultural one. The ancient formularies and, alas, even the new compositions, which try very hard to sound old and quaint, use a language that does not evoke contemporary images of life, and often does not correspond even to present-day religious thought. For instance, the opening prayers for the Masses at midnight and dawn of Christmas revolve around the image of light, a favorite theme of early composers. Christmas is the Christian version of the winter solstice celebration by Roman soldiers to honor the birth of the sun-god Mithras. Those who eagerly watch for the passing of the winter solstice, which today occurs a few days before 25 December, might find these prayers rather exciting, because of their reference to the victory of light over darkness. But to normal churchgoers the images suggested by Christmas are the manger, the angels, and the shepherds. These, by the way, are biblically rooted, whereas the connection between Christmas and the winter solstice is not. The theme of light is surely an all-time, cross-cultural favorite. But must we confine the Christmas imagery to it? Must our fidelity to one tradition require the sacrifice of a more biblical and contemporary Christmas imagery?

New alternative collects that are biblically inspired or bound to the current Sunday lectionary have adorned the Italian Sacramentary since 1983. The thinking behind this is that the collect introduces, in synthesis, the assigned theme of the Sunday readings, particularly the gospel. Whether or not this is the original purpose of the collect is debatable. But in the context of today's pastoral preoccupation for thematic celebrations (one need only think of such thematic Sunday Masses as "Mission Sunday," "Social Communications Sunday," and "Catechetical Sunday" to realize the extent of such preoccupation), biblically-bound collects are surely a progress in tradition. They answer a contemporary need. Another step forward is the revision of the English translation of the missal now being completed by the International Commission on English in the Liturgy. It promises not only greater fidelity to the Latin original (critics who attack the revised translation on this score should first consult the Latin text), but also closer attention to the components of contemporary English language, namely its thought, value, and rhetorical patterns (critics who attack the inclusive language used by this revised translation should be more sensitive to socio-cultural and linguistic evolution). This revised English missal is another progress in tradition.

We should add, however, that progress is not to be confined to the biblical and the linguistic components of liturgical texts. In traditionally Christian countries where popular religiosity has become part and parcel of people's faith-experience, the text should perhaps also reflect popular religious values and images associated with the feast. It is, of course, the liturgical text that largely determines how the feast is to be received and understood by the faithful. But there is absolutely no reason why the collect for Christmas should not speak about the baby in the crib, the song of the angels, and the shepherds. In some local churches of Spanish ancestry, Easter dawn witnesses the popular drama commemorating the "meeting" of the risen Christ with his mother, an apocryphal but profoundly devotional belief.[15] Where it is celebrated in conjunction with the morning

Mass, as part of the entrance rite, should not the collect in some way evoke the role of Christ's mother in the work of redemption? Evidently the gospel reading taken from John 20:1-9, which narrates the meeting between Christ and Mary Magdalene, has to be substituted, and the sequence, again about Mary Magdalene, dropped. When the prayer formularies are sensitive neither to the people's linguistic patterns nor to their popular religious expressions, there is little they can offer to enrich spiritual life. Progress in liturgy has also a pastoral dimension.

The General Instruction of the Roman Missal considers the eucharistic prayer "the center and summit of the entire celebration."[16] This seems to affirm indirectly the central position of transubstantiation which, in traditional theology, takes place at the words of consecration. In the Middle Ages and especially during the baroque period the moment of the consecration was regarded as the center and summit of the entire celebration: it is the moment when Christ's body and blood become present in sacramental form and the sacrifice of the cross is renewed in an unbloody manner. When the communion of the faithful became a rare occurrence, the moment of consecration was heightened even more by external manifestations such as the elevation, the use of incense, the ringing of church bells. What the Instruction seems to forget, however, is that the eucharistic prayer is not only an *actio sacrificii*, a sacrificial action, but a table blessing as well. It does not only make an *anamnesis* of Christ's sacrifice: it also prepares and leads to holy communion. Prayer before meals, however solemn and rich in doctrine, is surely not the center and summit of a meal. Unfortunately we have grown used to "communionless" Masses. When we do not sufficiently stress the meal aspect of the Mass, we will find it difficult to make the connection between the eucharistic prayer and communion.

The new Roman Missal offers as many as ten eucharistic prayers. The oldest, which has its origin in the fourth century, is the Roman Canon; the second, which has suffered from an overdose of corrections, is an adaptation of the anaphora contained in the third-century *Apostolic Tradition* attributed to St. Hippolytus of Rome; the fourth is inspired by the Alexandrian anaphora of St. Basil; the rest are contemporary compositions.[17]

The question that can be raised here comes from a cultural concern and is in the interest of intelligent participation. Do these ten eucharistic prayers correspond to any people's established patterns of praising and thanking God for God's gifts, particularly of food and drink? Are these prayers evocative of the institutions, traditions, and life experience of any given community? In short, if people are taught that these prayers are solemn table prayers, will they identify them as such and claim them as their own? Liturgical prayers, we are told, are "the prayer of some actual community, assembled here and now."[18] The difficulty is that these prayers were composed in another age and for another people, or alas with no particular group of people in mind. This is why, they can hardly be considered "the prayer of some actual community, assembled here and now." In fact, of the ten eucharistic prayers in the missal only one can be said to address directly a particular assembly and allude to actual linguistic and value patterns: the fourth-century Roman Canon.

The matter becomes even more problematic when these prayers are translated. A person who possesses a keen appreciation of the rhetorical quality of the Roman Canon knows that it defies translation. It was not meant to be translated, anyway. However accurate and literary the translation, it will not be able to convey the cultural milieu in which the prayer had originally been written. At any rate, we know that that milieu is lost in the mist of history, nor is it wholesome to pretend that the liturgical assembly of our time shares the Roman cultural genius that adorns the Roman Canon. On the other hand, the new eucharistic prayers were composed with the understanding that they would be translated into different living languages. They did not grow from any cultural milieu, and they were written in the Latin of teachers and scholars, which does not mean that their Latin is of inferior quality but that it does not exhibit the traits of the classical liturgical language of Rome. With due respect for their authors, it must be said that these prayers sound better in translation. Yet however perfect the translation, these texts seem foreign: they do not seem to be "the prayer of some actual community, assembled here and now."

Perhaps in view of this difficulty, the Congregation for Divine Worship informed the conferences of bishops as early as 1973 that the "Apostolic See will accord every consideration to the petitions submitted by the conferences of bishops for the possible composition in special circumstances of a new eucharistic prayer and its introduction into the liturgy."[19] Would it not indeed be a major step forward in liturgical tradition if every local church were to have a particular eucharistic prayer that expresses the richness and variety of culture and traditions? For too long we have been made to believe that in the liturgy what was good in the past must also be good for the present even without adaptations, and that what was composed in view of no particular community must be the right thing for every particular community. Liturgical tradition does not consist of keeping the past intact and as if it were unsullied; rather it means being guided by the past. Composing prayers that speak to people and about the life and faith experience of people is part of liturgical tradition.

Another aspect of the Missal of Paul VI that can be discussed here is the question of ritualization. Gestures in the liturgy always tend to acquire a symbolic meaning, including those that originally had been purely practical in nature, like the washing of hands at the offertory rite. When we sit, kneel, or stand, we not only add intensity to the word, but also arouse and express the deeper feelings of our heart as well as our collective experience of God, the church, and the world. This is why, for liturgical symbols to be effective means of communicating the reality of the Christian mystery, they have to be inscribed in people's culture and traditions. Unassimilated symbols borrowed from another people can become mimicry. Rightly, the General Instruction of the Roman Missal allows "the conferences of bishops to adapt the actions and postures described in the Order of Mass to the customs of the people," provided "such adaptations correspond to the meaning and character of each part of the celebration."[20]

In their eagerness to rid the missal of medieval accretions, particularly of the Franco-Germanic type, the postconciliar revisors eliminated a good number of symbols. Simplification through elimination was the order of the day. Perhaps it was the right thing to do. After all, in the Roman liturgy "less is more," while the accumulation of symbols can cause the same cloying feeling one gets in a profusely and elaborately ornamented rococo church. Furthermore, certain symbols in the Missal of Pius V, like the transfer of the missal from the epistle to the gospel side, have become irrelevant ever since the ambo was restored. What has happened, though, is that contemporary symbols have not replaced the old, new ones have not been introduced to fill the vacuum. We know that the liturgy has an *horror vacui*; it does not easily tolerate a *lacuna* of symbols.

It seems that we are being parsimonious in the use of symbols and gestures, especially for the eucharistic prayer. Why is it, for example, that the consecratory epiclesis has a special gesture, namely the handlaying on bread and wine, whereas the communion epiclesis has none? The Roman Canon has been allowed to keep several traditional gestures. The presider bows at the words *supplices te rogamus;* he signs himself with the cross while reciting *omni benedictione caelesti;* he beats his breast while praying *nobis quoque peccatoribus.* Why are these gestures missing in the other eucharistic prayers? Surely these are medieval accretions, whereas the classical posture of the presider at the eucharistic prayer seems to have been limited to extending his arms and raising the eucharistic elements at the final doxology. But in cultures that tend to be expressive more with bodily gestures than with words the simplicity of the rite for the new eucharistic prayers is equivalent to ritual poverty.

Perhaps to make up for the economy of symbols (or is it because of our propensity to communicate orally?), we tend to overload the celebration with words. It is quite regrettable that the revised Missal of Paul VI has overreacted to its predecessor's profuse symbolism, forgetting that the liturgy not only speaks words but also employs nonverbal communication. The extent to which words are used during Mass is symptomatic of a verbal overdose. Before the Mass begins the commentator reads the theme and the intentions; after the greeting the presider gives a prehomiletic *fervorino;* before each reading the commentator reads the exegetical background of the biblical passage and a spiritual exhortation. The rest of the Mass is, of course, made up of readings and formularies. Alas, some eucharistic liturgies have been converted into a barrage of long-winded prayers and an endless outpouring of words.

Besides the foregoing ritual elements there are others that need to be reviewed in the light of their origin and actual usefulness. One of these is the penitential rite whose origin goes back to the ninth-century *Ordo VI* and the tenth-century *Ordo X.*

These *ordines* or rubrical books for the celebration of Mass exhort the priest to confess his own sins before he celebrates, in the manner of one who approaches the "penitential tribunal." In the tenth century when the Mass became one of the easy, though somewhat expensive, ways to commute the heavy satisfaction imposed on the penitent, the practice of reciting the apologies became part of the entrance rite of the Mass.[21] The Missal of Pius V adopted the longest form of this apology consisting of the *Confiteor* or the formulary "I confess" at the beginning of Mass and the entire Psalm 43. We observe that the origin of this rite is rooted in the penitential discipline of the Middle Ages as well as in the spiritual and perhaps cultural inclination of the Franco-Germanic people to reiterate their condition of unworthiness.

The Missal of Paul VI adds a novelty having no historical precedence. The penitential rite, which had always been a private prayer of the presider though with the assistance of the server, was made into a prayer of the entire assembly. Some think it is a timely spiritual reminder, and hence should be a normal starter, especially on Sundays when people are present in greater number. Performed daily, it can become a routine. In the light of its history, what value should we give to the penitential rite on which the church is reticent to confer any sacramental value? And in the light of the liturgical year, what meaning does it have on Sunday, particularly during Easter season? Does it not jeopardize the joy that should distinguish the celebration of the Lord's Day? The penitential rite is, of course, not the same as doing penance, like fasting and praying on one's knees, which the early Church Fathers forbade on Sunday. Yet the tenor of the rite is what it is called: *penitential.* Furthermore, while it is true that penance should characterize the entire life of Christians, must we almost always begin the Mass with the penitential rite? Unfortunately the rite of sprinkling at Sunday Masses in remembrance of baptism is, perhaps because of the time it consumes, still a rather rare occurrence.

If the above arguments are not convincing, perhaps something more creative than the simple recitation of the penitential formularies could be considered for Sundays in Lent. For example, one could transform the entrance procession into a penitential procession during which the *Kyrie* with its invocations is chanted. Assemblies with propensity for dramatic effect might find the use of a large crucifix carried aloft by the presider meaningful. Popular traditions connected with penitential processions might be able to provide some useful elements. There is no reason why the entrance procession should always be carried out with the magnificence it had during the time of Constantine. One may call into question the idea of a penitential procession at Sunday Masses even during Lent. Yet the Lenten liturgy itself sets the example by silencing the organ, dropping the *Gloria*, and using purple color.

But a more pointed question is whether the Mass always needs an introductory rite, especially of a type whose components are hopelessly disparate: entrance song, sign of the cross, greeting, introductory words, rite of sprinkling or penitential rite in one of the three forms, *Kyrie* if this is not part of the penitential rite, *Gloria*, and collect. In some places, as we have noted earlier, the commentator may also give a preview of the readings. By the time the introductory rite is over, one can only sigh with relief. It is interesting to know that we have record of an Easter Sunday Mass celebrated by St. Augustine, in which the only introduction was the greeting: "I greeted the people and they began to cry out in their enthusiasm. When silence was restored, the readings from sacred scripture were proclaimed."[22] Whether or not this was the normal procedure in Hippo is difficult to determine. The absence of an entrance rite proper could have been motivated by the preceding night's lengthy vigil or the commotion caused by the cure of a young man that Sunday morning before the Mass began.

Another element of the Roman Mass that calls for review is the venerable hymn *Gloria*. An ancient hymn used in the Byzantine Churches for morning prayer, it became, for still unknown reason, a component of the Roman entrance rite toward the sixth century. Until the eleventh century it was sung only at pontifical Masses on Christmas, Sundays, and feasts of martyrs.[23] The question is, what is it doing at the entrance rite? Is it in the right place, or would it be more meaningful if it were relocated elsewhere, say right after the greeting as an opening hymn, distinct from the song that accompanies the entrance procession, or perhaps after communion as a kind of thanksgiving hymn? If it is not sung, would it still be necessary to recite it? How do we justify the recitation of a hymn? But it seems that a more basic question is whether the *Gloria* has a place at all in the celebration of Mass. Is its antiquity enough reason to keep it there?

We can raise similar questions regarding the recitation of the profession of faith at Mass. The General Instruction on the Roman Missal gives what seems to be a lame justification of the practice: it "serves as a way for the people to respond and to give their assent to the word of God heard in the readings and through the homily, and for them to call to mind the truths of faith before they begin to celebrate the eucharist."[24] At Masses when it is not recited, how do people respond and give their assent to the word of God? How do they, on such occasions, call to mind the truths of faith? History tells us that the profession of faith was originally a part of the baptismal liturgy only, not of the Mass. History also tells us that the profession was introduced into the liturgy of Constantinople in the sixth century as a check against heresies. In 1014 Emperor Henry II of Spain wanted to introduce it into the Roman Mass, there being no reason why Rome, of all the churches, was the only one that did not recite it. The proud Roman clergy objected on grounds that the Roman Church, unlike the other churches, had not been infected with heresy.[25]

Since the profession of faith is more properly linked to baptism than to the eucharistic celebration, a possibility would be—if it is considered integral to Sunday Masses—to incorporate it into the rite of sprinkling, perhaps using the question and answer form. In this way the rite of sprinkling will be more evocative of baptism. In this way too the profession of faith will be in place as a baptismal element rather than an anti-heretical formula or in the present thinking a response to the word of God in the form of a dogmatic statement.

Another element that can be re-examined here is the sign of peace which the earlier documents were not embarrassed to describe as a kiss. We should note though that a later tradition specified that "the clergy embrace the bishop, laymen embrace laymen, and laywomen embrace laywomen."[26] The meaning of the sign has been interpreted in different ways, depending on its location in the Order of Mass. It is well-known that in the time of Tertullian the kiss was exchanged after the prayer of the faithful. It is for this reason that he calls it *signaculum orationis*.[27] On the other hand, in the time of St. Augustine the kiss of peace was

given before communion as a preparatory rite: *pacis signum est.*
This is the meaning generally attached to it today.[28] In Rome, at
the time of Pope Innocent I, the rite of peace concluded, as it
were, the recitation of the eucharistic prayer. Hence, he regarded it as some kind of *signaculum eucharistiae.*[29] In the Zairean
Mass the sign of peace comes after the penitential rite, which
follows the liturgy of the word. In this context, it acquires a new
meaning, namely reconciliation. We may call it the *signaculum
reconciliationis.*[30]

The manner of giving the sign has also undergone significant
variations: real and genuine kiss, formal and stiff embrace, kissing a large medal passed among the clergy, and today in some
places a nod of greeting with or even without a smile or the
multivalent handshake. When a western missionary imposed
the handshake as sign of peace, he could not quite comprehend
why the assembly found the rite so funny as the word "con-
gratulations!" was passed around. The General Instruction of
the Roman Missal allows conferences of bishops to determine
the manner of giving the sign of peace "in accord with the
culture and customs of the people."[31] Given the various mean-
ings of the sign of peace and the ways of doing it, how are we to
understand and perform the rite? The fundamental questions
are, when should the sign of peace be given, and should it be
given at all everyday? Since the eucharistic celebration is an
unbroken unit, though with distinct components, and the sign
of peace is generally understood today as sign of fellowship not
merely in communion but also in the entire celebration, might it
not be more meaningful to give it at the beginning of the Mass?
Its present location, before communion, comes rather late in
terms of acknowledging each other's presence, and in effusive
assemblies its equally effusive performance can create a discon-
certing feeling, considering the presence of the sacred species on
the altar. Must it be done everyday? In daily assemblies made
up of regular participants the frequency of the sign can cause it
to become routine. At any rate, the sign is not obligatory but *pro
opportunitate.*

* * * * * * * *

When Pope Paul VI introduced innovations in the monolithic
Missal of Pius V, he did not sin against liturgical tradition nor

did he ignore it. Rather he affirmed that sound tradition is always open to legitimate progress. When he abandoned certain medieval traditions, he showed that liturgical traditions are valid and meaningful only as they are able to answer the needs of contemporary local churches. When he restored liturgical practices in accord with the "tradition of the Fathers" both eastern and western, he declared that the church possesses not one but several traditions. Pope Paul VI was not an iconoclast, but he did not want to enshrine every tradition regardless of its usefulness to the church.

Some traditions, if they are updated to suit the present, may prove useful even today. Others, on the other hand, may have to be discontinued if they no longer speak to people. The important thing to keep in mind is that the church not only conserves traditions, it also improves them, like the faithful servant to whom the Master has entrusted the talents. And there are occasions when the church, under the inspiration of the Holy Spirit and out of pastoral concern for local communities, discards old traditions and starts new ones. Liturgical traditions do not come exclusively from the remote past, from the Apostles and the Church Fathers. They are continually being created by the church, because the Holy Spirit is never content with maintaining the *status quo*. After all, do we not constantly ask the Holy Spirit to "renew the face of the earth"?

Perhaps there is no better way of concluding this chapter than by recalling what the General Instruction of the Roman Missal[32] has so forcefully proclaimed: "The Church remains faithful in her responsibility as teacher of truth to guard 'things old', that is, the deposit of tradition; at the same time she fulfills another duty, that of examining and prudently bringing forth 'things new' (Mt 13:52)."

Notes

1. Paul VI, Apostolic Constitution *Missale Romanum, Missale Romanum*, editio typica altera (Vatican City, 1975) 12; English translation in *Documents on the Liturgy*, henceforth DOL (Collegeville, 1982) 456.

2. Constitution on the Sacred Liturgy (SC) art. 50; English translation in DOL 14.

3. *Le Sacramentaire grégorien*, vol. 1, ed. J. Deshusses (Fribourg, 1979) 85-92.

4. Paul VI, Apostolic Constitution *Missale Romanum*, DOL 459.

5. SC 51, DOL 14.

6. General Instruction on the Roman Missal (GIRM), Prooemium, no. 6, p. 22; DOL 467.

7. See C. Vogel, *Medieval Liturgy: An Introduction to the Sources* (Washington, D.C., 1986) 208-209.

8. *De Sacramentis* IV, 23, ed. B. Botte, Sources chrétiennes, vol. 25bis (Paris, 1961) 114.

9. GIRM 8-9, DOL 467.

10. GIRM 10, DOL 467.

11. See J. Jungmann, *The Mass of the Roman Rite*, 2 vols. (Westminster MD, 1951); R. Cabié, *The Eucharist*, vol. 2 of *The Church at Prayer* (Collegeville, 1986); H. Meyer, *Eucharistie*, in *Gottesdienst der Kirche* (Regensburg, 1989); A. Nocent, "Storia della celebrazione dell'eucaristia," *Anamnesis*, vol. 3:2 (Genoa, 1989) 189-270.

12. For studies and recommendations concerning future revisions of the present missal, see: A. Nocent, *Liturgia Semper Reformanda* (Magnano 1993) 9-68; F. McManus, "The Roman Order of Mass from 1964 to 1969: The Preparation of the Gifts," *Worship* 65 (1991) 107-138; M. Searle, "Semper Reformanda: The Opening and Closing Rites of the Mass," in *Shaping English Liturgy* (Washington, D.C., 1990) 53-92; T. Krosnicki, "Grace and Peace: Greeting the Assembly," ibid. 93-106.

13. See A. Dumas, "Les sources du nouveau missel romain," *Notitiae* 7 (1971) 37-42. The author also indicates the sources for other non-Roman prayers in the new missal.

14. A. Nocent, "Storia della celebrazione dell'eucaristia," *Anamnesis*, vol. 3:2, 205-208.

15. A. Chupungco: *Liturgical Inculturation: Sacramentals, Religiosity, and Catechesis* (Collegeville, 1992) 100-118.

16. GIRM 54, DOL 481.

17. E. Mazza, *The Eucharistic Prayers of the Roman Rite* (New York, 1986); Meyer, *Eucharistie* 348-352.

18. Consilium, Instruction *Come le prévoit* 20, DOL 287.

19. Congregation for Divine Worship, Circular Letter *Eucharistiae Participationem* 6, DOL 625. Three eucharistic prayers approved for particular churches are the "Swiss" (whose use has been extended to the entire Latin rite), the "Canadian" for marriage, and the "Zairean."

20. GIRM 21, DOL 474.

21. A. Nocent, "Les apologies dans la célébration eucharistique," *Liturgie et rémission des péchés* (Rome, 1975) 179-196.

22. Augustine, *De Civitate Dei*, 22,8, Corpus Christianorum, vol. 48 (Turnhout, 1955) 826; see Cabié, *The Eucharist* 50-51.

23. Cabié, *The Eucharist* 204-205.

24. GIRM 43, DOL 479.

25. A. Nocent, "Storia della celebrazione dell'eucaristia" 216-217.

26. Ibid. 263-265; Cabié, *The Eucharist* 113-155.

27. Tertullian, *De Oratione* 18, Corpus Christianorum, vol. 1:1 (1954) 267.

28. Augustine, *Sermo* 227, Sources chrétiennes, vol. 116, 240.

29. Innocent I, *Epistola 25 ad Decentium* 1,4, PL 20:267; see A. Nocent, "Storia della celebrazione dell'eucaristia" 263-264.

30. *Rite zaïrois de la célébration eucharistique* (Kinshasa, 1985).

31. GIRM 56b, DOL 483.

32. GIRM no. 15, DOL 469.

6

Toward a Ferial Order of Mass

FOR OVER TWENTY YEARS WE HAVE BEEN CELEBRATING THE EUCHARIST according to the Order of Mass published by Pope Paul VI in 1970. One gets the impression that regardless of the rank of the feast or the season of the liturgical year, the same Order of Mass as on weekdays is followed, except for a couple of added features like the *Gloria*, a second reading, and the creed. But one may also get the opposite impression, and this is the correct one, that the Order of Mass on weekdays is a slightly simplified version of the one we use on Sundays and feast days. The fact is, we do not have a ferial Order of Mass. We make do with what exists which, as we shall see later on, was meant in the first place for Sunday celebrations. The long and short of it is that we celebrate on weekdays what properly belongs to Sunday. This reminds us of a similar situation. Until 1969 there had never been a rite of baptism prepared specifically for children. We know that the rite of infant baptism published by Pope Paul V in 1614 was nothing more than a shorter form of the rite of baptism for adults.

THE CONCEPT OF FESTIVE LITURGY

There is today a growing sensitivity to the progressive solemnity in liturgical celebrations. The higher the rank of a feast, the greater its solemnity or festive character. Certain days of the liturgical year call for greater liturgical solemnity. Article 102 of the Constitution on the Liturgy (SC) gives the reason for this. There are days to which the church has assigned particular aspects of Christ's saving work: these are feast days and are celebrated as such. The connection between feast day and festive liturgy is clear: "The Church is conscious that it must celebrate the saving work of the divine Bridegroom by devoutly recalling it on certain days throughout the course of the year." Sunday is obviously one such day. On this day the church "keeps the memory of the Lord's resurrection, which it also celebrates once in the year, together with his blessed passion, in the most solemn festival of Easter." The Constitution attaches such importance to Sunday, as the Lord's Day, that other feasts, unless they are truly of greatest importance, may not have precedence over it.

We may apply the principle of progressive solemnity also to the other feasts of the Lord, for they unfold the whole mystery of Christ, from his incarnation to the day of Pentecost (SC 102). The same is true of the feasts of the Blessed Virgin Mary, the martyrs, and other saints, since in their own way these feasts also proclaim the paschal mystery (SC 103-104). The Constitution likewise makes the provision that "the Proper of Seasons shall be given the precedence due to it over the feasts of the saints, in order that the entire cycle of the mysteries of salvation may be celebrated in the measure due to them" (SC 108). All of the above are festive days because they recall aspects of Christ's mystery, though in various ways and degrees.

It seems therefore that the Constitution develops the concept of feast from the connection it sees between the liturgical day or season and one or other aspect of Christ's saving work. The postconciliar calendar invokes this concept when it speaks of the Easter triduum, the seasons of Easter, Lent, Christmas and Advent, and Ordinary Time as the yearly cycle whereby the church celebrates the whole mystery of Christ. The calendar distinguishes Ordinary Time from the other seasons. Unlike these, which have their own distinctive character, the weeks in Ordinary Time "do not celebrate a specific aspect of the mystery of Christ. Rather, especially on Sundays, they are devoted to the mystery of Christ in all its aspects."[1]

The principle is not entirely new. Tertullian tells us that "Easter is the solemn day for baptism, because it is the day when the passion of the Lord, in which we are washed, was accomplished."[2] He extends this to the other days from Easter to Pentecost, for these are regarded as one day of feasting. He does not, of course, exclude the other days of the year, in as much as "every day belongs to the Lord," and hence any hour and any time is suitable for baptism. The difference, he explains, does not lie in the grace received but in the solemnity of the celebration: *si de sollemnitate interest, de gratia nihil refert*.[3] However, liturgy is not confined to the reception of grace; its nature as a public act of the church necessarily involves ritual form. It is true that the content of the sacraments, whether they are celebrated on Sunday or a weekday, is the same, but their outward form, which includes time dimension, spells a great deal of difference. Every day belongs to the Lord, but not every day calls for solemn celebration or festivity, because not every day commemorates and celebrates a particular aspect of Christ's mystery. Not every day is a feast.

The Constitution on the Liturgy develops the notion of a festive or solemn celebration in ways that are quite different from the traditional understanding of what a solemn liturgy is all about. Its premises are theological rather than rubrical, namely the nature of the worshiping community and the liturgical year. As regards the worshiping community the Constitution lists in the first place the eucharistic celebrations, especially in the cathedral church, at which the bishop presides, surrounded by his college of presbyters and by his assistants, and in which the people participate fully and actively (SC 41). Such celebrations, which we may call episcopal (pontifical suggests ceremonies), the Constitution regards as the "preeminent manifestation of the Church." They are comparable to the Roman stational Mass of the bishop, which is, "as it were, the model of all liturgies." The early eighth-century *Ordo Romanus I* describes in great detail an impressive papal stational Mass on Easter Sunday.[4]

We conclude from this that the liturgy has a festive character when the bishop in the company of his clergy presides at the eucharistic celebration in which the people participate. This form of episcopal liturgy is by nature festive or solemn. Although it normally takes place on Sunday or an important feast day, it should still be considered a festive celebration when held for exceptional reasons on a weekday.

In the spirit of the Constitution on the Sacred Liturgy (42), the General Instruction of the Roman Missal presents a presbyteral form which is derived from the episcopal. These are the Masses celebrated by any community but especially by a parish community. The stress here seems to be principally on the community assembled for the Sunday eucharist. The General Instruction calls this a "Mass with a Congregation" at which "as a rule an acolyte, a reader, and a cantor assist the celebrating priest." This form of celebration allows an even greater number of ministers: thurifer, candlebearers, crossbearer, acolytes, reader, and deacon if there is one. All are clad in their respective vestments. All and sundry contribute to the solemnity of the occasion. This form of the Mass, the General Instruction tells us, represents the *forma typica* or the basic, typical form of the eucharistic celebration, and hence, as far as possible, and especially on Sundays and holidays of obligation, should be celebrated with song. Yet it may also be celebrated without music and with only one minister.[5]

This last provision is remarkably odd for "Mass with a Congregation." It strikes a jarring note in the musical reform of Vatican II. The Constitution on the Liturgy considers liturgical music "a necessary or integral part of the solemn liturgy" (SC 112), observing that "a liturgical service takes a nobler aspect when the rites are celebrated in singing, the sacred ministers take their parts in them, and the faithful actively participate" (SC 113). The possibility of celebrating without any song the "Mass with a Congregation," however small the assembly might be, faithfully but sadly reflects a proposed emendation to the *Missa normativa* made during the 1967 Synod of Bishops: "The read Mass and not the sung Mass should be normative; it is easier to celebrate a read Mass on Sundays and feast days."[6]

It might be useful at this point to remember that the *Missa normativa* is the immediate predecessor of the present *forma typica* of the Order of Mass. A. Bugnini explains that "the Mass was called 'normative' because, while there would always be several forms of celebration, this was the one that was to serve as the norm or standard for the others." The study group that met in 1964 to prepare the new Order of Mass defined the *Missa normativa* as a "Mass celebrated by a priest, with a reader, servers, a choir or cantor, and a congregation." The idea was to make a sharper distinction between Mass "in private" or without a congregation and Mass with a congregation. Furthermore, the group initially insisted that the sung, not the read, Mass was to be the model. Obviously this type of Mass, unlike the one without a congregation, would require areas for the altar, lectern, presidential chair, and perhaps fewer formularies, "since by its nature its celebration will take more time."[7]

Thus the festive character of a "Mass with a Congregation" is determined chiefly by the presence of an assembly which "represents the universal Church gathered at a given time and place." The General Instruction adds that the attribution of a universal character to the liturgical assembly is particularly true when it celebrates the Lord's Day.[8] This ecclesiological consideration alone should suffice to explain why such gatherings are festive. What gives a solemn or festive quality to the Sunday eucharist is, in the final analysis, the participation of the assembly. This is why, strictly speaking, the "Mass with a Congregation" can be celebrated on Sunday without music and with only one minister, and yet be festive. Community, eucharist, and Sunday: these are the three components of a festive or solemn presbyteral liturgy. The "Mass with a Congregation," as we shall see presently, had been shaped with the Sunday assembly in mind. Nothing is mentioned in the General Instruction regarding ferial Masses, although it implies that the typical form of "Masses with a Congregation" applies to them as well.

The other premise on which the Constitution on the Liturgy bases its notion of a festive celebration is the theology of the liturgical year. We come across frequent references to this in the chapter on liturgical year and in other articles of the Constitution: art. 42 (parish Sunday Mass), art. 53 (general intercessions on Sundays and holydays of obligation), and art. 100 (Sunday lauds and vespers). A liturgy is festive not only when the bishop, his presbyters, and the community are present, but also when it is celebrated on Sunday or a feast day. Liturgical books have traditionally been very attentive to this. Our early and medieval sources offer detailed information on how the Mass was celebrated by the bishop on feast days and special occasions. But we possess little information on how it was celebrated by presbyters on Sundays. We presume that at least the entrance rite even on Sunday would have been much simpler than what *Ordo Romanus I* describes for the papal liturgy.[9]

Sunday played a considerable role in shaping the "Mass with a Congregation." In this connection A. Bugnini's account of how the *Missa normativa* took the shape it has today is very enlightening. When it was celebrated at the 1967 Synod of Bishops, the understanding was that "the Mass was to be thought of as a Sunday Mass in a parish church with the participation of a congregation, a small choir, a lector, a cantor, and two servers."[10] Some Synod Fathers were quite overwhelmed by the solemnity of the celebration and remarked that it was not practicable in ordinary parishes. The point is that Sunday as the Lord's Day deserves to be celebrated with some degree of solemnity. For this reason, the definition of the *Missa normativa*, which was meant to be a Sunday celebration, "was to be based on Mass with singing, a reader, at least one server, a choir or cantor, and a congregation."[11] The "Mass with a Congregation" retains these essential features of the *Missa normativa*. A brief glance at this "basic form of celebration" which supposes a host of ministers clad in their vestments, not to mention the lighted candles, incense, processional cross, and the Book of the Gospels, tells us that we are dealing here with a typical form of Sunday eucharist. The form for the daily celebration is passed over in silence. This is surely a lacuna in the liturgical reform of Vatican II.

In summary we may identify the chief elements that constitute a festive liturgy. These are: the celebrations, especially of the eucharist, presided by the bishop; the typical form called "Mass with a Congregation"; and the time elements of Sunday and other days to which liturgy has assigned a feast or a special celebration. On such days and occasions the liturgy assumes a festive or solemn character.

A RECONSTRUCTION OF THE FERIAL LITURGY

If there are days that call for greater solemnity because they are feasts, there are others that do not because they are not feasts. In liturgical tradition such days came to be known as ferial days, when no particular aspect of Christ's mystery is recalled or when no feast of a saint is celebrated. Except for an implicit reference to ferial days in connection with the Proper of Seasons, the Constitution on the Liturgy does not mention the other ferial days of the liturgical year. We should not be surprised by this. The chief concern of the Constitution is to ensure that the entire mystery of Christ is unfolded during the year through liturgical celebrations, especially the Mass, and for this it sets apart Sundays, feasts, and liturgical seasons. Tradition, however, is firm on the existence of weekday or ferial Masses.[12]

It would seem that the notion of a ferial day in liturgical usage is less akin to the primary meaning of the Latin *feriae* (holidays, festivals) than to its transferred sense of being idle or disengaged. This does not in any case exclude the possibility that the liturgical ferial days and the naming of the weekdays from Monday to Friday as *feriae* originated in the *feriae* or holidays that characterized the Easter week.[13] We may say that a liturgical day is considered ferial when it is "free" from any allotment, that is, when no feast, anniversary, or special celebration is attached to it. Hence a weekday on which one of these occurs is not regarded as ferial but feast day. Perhaps Ash Wednesday and the days of Holy Week are an exception to this, since the former has a special rite and the latter recalls in a general way the passion of the Lord. Nonetheless, the calendar does not list them as feasts but as ferial days.

The General Norms for the Liturgical Year and the Calendar, which defines ferial days quite simply as "the days following Sunday," distinguishes three categories. Under the first are Ash Wednesday and the days of Holy Week from Monday to Thursday inclusive. These ferial days have precedence over all other celebrations. Under the second are the weekdays of Advent from 17 to 24 December inclusive and all the weekdays of Lent. They have precedence over obligatory memorials. And under the third are all other weekdays. They give way to solemnities and feasts and are combined with memorials.[14] As feasts are ranked according to importance, so are ferial days—five of which are superior to any solemnity or feast. The rest are either preferred to obligatory memorials or are combined with memorials. What the system of precedence seems to say is that ferial days should not be deemed unimportant in the overall plan of the liturgical year. These "free" days permit us to listen in the course of the year to a wider variety of readings from Sacred Scripture than feasts can offer, especially now that we have a ferial lectionary. In fact the Missal of Pius V kept around 150 days free for the same reason, though its ferial lectionary is confined to the season of Lent and the ember days.[15] Furthermore, the nature of the liturgical year requires a healthy balance between feasts and ferial days. It is both liturgically and humanly difficult to cope with the demands of daily festivity.

We note in passing that the precedence some ferial days enjoy over feasts does not suggest that we solemnize them. Liturgical precedence does not turn them into solemnities or feasts. They are ferial days and there is no reason why the Mass, even on high-ranking ferial days, should be celebrated with the full complement reserved for Sunday "Mass with a Congregation."

But what shape should the Mass have on ferial days? Before the episcopal liturgy described in *Ordo Romanus I* became the standard, though reduced, form even for daily Masses, do we possess information on the shape of the ferial Order of Mass? Pope Gregory the Great speaks of *Missae cotidianae* or daily Masses. These he contrasts with Sunday Masses in connection with the litanies that precede the acclamations *Kyrie-Christe eleison*. The litanies are not said in daily Masses, and "we recite only *Kyrie eleison* and *Christe eleison*." Apart from this he mentions nothing about the structure of daily Masses.[16] However, if we take into account that at his time there had as yet been no penitential rite and the *Gloria* was sung only on Sunday if the bishop was presiding, the entrance rite for weekday Masses by presbyters could very well have consisted only of a greeting, *Kyrie-Christe* acclamations (without the litanies), the *Oremus* followed by a silent pause, and the collect. Since presbyters were not welcomed with a song, unlike the bishops who enjoyed this privilege which imitated the imperial court ceremonial, there would have been no entrance song at presbyteral Masses even on Sunday.[17]

The Gregorian Sacramentary sent by Pope Hadrian I to Charlemagne toward the end of the eighth century contains a short Order of Mass suitable for both festive and ferial celebrations: *sive diebus festis seu cottidianis.*[18] Although this Sacramentary was for the use of the pope, its Order of Mass, taking cognizance of the fact that presbyters presided at the eucharist on Sundays and ferial days, makes references to the *presbyter* or *sacerdos*. Is this an indication that at least by the eighth century the papal ceremonies of *Ordo Romanus I* were already being adopted, though in a reduced measure, for the presbyteral Mass?[19] The Sacramentary informs us that the *introitum* varies on given days depending on whether it is a feast or a ferial day. The *Kyrie eleison* is said, followed by the *Gloria*, but only on Sunday and if a bishop presides. On days of fast neither the *Gloria* nor the *Alleluia* is sung. After the collect come the reading from the Apostle, the gradual psalm or *Alleluia*, and the gospel. Then follow the offertory rite with the prayer over the gifts, the Canon, the Lord's Prayer with embolism, the greeting of peace, and the *Agnus Dei*. The Sacramentary ends here its description of this festive-ferial Order of Mass.

Does this scanty information allow us to conclude or at least presume that other elements of the Sunday Mass were omitted during weekdays? Are we permitted to apply to the other parts of the Mass what Pope Gregory says about the entrance litanies: *alia quae dici solent tacemus*? Guesswork is even less fruitful here. Since the festive episcopal liturgy is the basis for our work of reconstructing the shape of the ferial Mass, the most that can be said is that the presbyter would have omitted what pertained to the rank of the bishop, at least until that time in the Middle Ages when the papal ceremonies of *Ordo Romanus I* were used for presbyteral Masses as well.

Which elements of the eucharistic liturgy were regarded at the time of *Ordo Romanus I* as properly episcopal or more precisely papal? *Ordo Romanus II*, a contemporary Roman supplement to *Ordo Romanus I*, supplies us with relevant, though meager, information on this. Since it regulates the celebration of the stational Masses by a bishop or a presbyter whenever the pope is unable to preside, it indicates the adaptations to be made on papal ceremonies. Some of these are: the celebrant does not use the papal throne; the archdeacon does not raise the chalice at the doxology of the eucharistic prayer; the first commingling is done with the *fermentum* from the bread previously consecrated by the pope himself rather than with the *Sancta* or consecrated bread kept in the church; the second breaking of bread is done not at the throne but at the altar; and even at stational Masses at which a presbyter presides the *Gloria* is omitted, because it is not to be said by presbyters except on Easter day.[20] *Ordo Romanus II*, being a stational Order of Mass, is not typical for the presbyteral Masses on Sundays and much less weekdays. However, it does tell us that certain elements of the eucharistic celebration are reserved to positions of higher rank. This is a premise on which the presbyteral liturgy rests.

As regards the formularies for weekday Masses the Gelasian Sacramentary and Benedict of Aniane's Supplement to the Gregorian-Hadrian Sacramentary each contains six sets of formularies that carry the title *Orationes cotidianis diebus ad Missas* or in short, for ferial Masses.[21] The presence of the three formularies, namely the collect, prayer over the gifts, and prayer after communion, assures us that these were recited at daily Masses.

Another detail worth pursuing is the chanting of the *Alleluia*. Most codices of *Ordo Romanus I* instruct the cantor to sing the *Alleluia* after the responsorial psalm (*responsum* or *gradale*), unless a tract (*tractus*) has to replace it, obviously during Lent. But there are other times, and these can refer only to ferial days, when neither the *Alleluia* nor the *tractus* is sung, although the responsorial psalm is.[22] This psalm would appear to be a normal part of the liturgy of the word and would have been sung even on those days when the *Alleluia* was omitted. Does it mean that the weekday Masses always had a responsorial psalm, but not the *Alleluia* or the tract? We wrestle with a difficult material. However, it is not impossible to catch a glimpse of what could have been a ferial Order of Mass before the episcopal was made the standard form for every eucharistic celebration.

The fact that ferial days are "free" made them easily susceptible of the developments in eucharistic theology and spirituality. Especially during the Middle Ages, when Masses were celebrated for reasons of personal devotion and impetration, ferial days became the normal days for votive Masses or Masses for various needs (early sacramentaries do not distinguish between these two types of Masses). For the month of October the Veronese Sacramentary offers a set of formularies "in time of drought."[23] The Gelasian Sacramentary has over sixty formularies for this type of Masses, which reveal something of the eucharistic spirituality of the period. Whether each set corresponded to a ferial day is not clear.[24] Similarly, the Supplement to the Gregorian-Hadrian Sacramentary includes a great number of

Mass formularies for various needs: for peace, in time of pestilence, for rain, for fine weather, for travellers, and so on.[25] The medieval practice of celebrating votive Masses and certain Masses for various needs on "free" days of the week is carried over today, though with a good measure of restraint.[26]

Tradition has known other types of the eucharistic celebration aside from the episcopal and the Sunday "Mass with a Congregation." These are the Masses celebrated at home (*Missa domestica*), with a small group, in private (*Missa privata* with one minister), with neither a congregation nor a minister (*Missa solitaria*), outside the monastic conventual Mass (*Missa matutinalis*), for the dead (*De requie*), in honor of the Blessed Virgin Mary (*De Beata*), and for the commutation of penance (*redemptiones paenitentiales*).[27] These types of Masses are related to the *Missae cotidianae*, and more often than not were celebrated on weekdays and hence with less ritual elaboration. Yet it would not be exact to identify all of them with the ferial Masses mentioned by Pope Gregory I, since some could have easily been celebrated on Sundays and feast days at home or with a small group or even in private. In other words, the names of these Masses do not tell us that they were necessarily *Missae cotidianae* using a ferial Order.

To sum up, we may define ferial liturgy by contrasting it with the festive. A liturgical celebration is ferial on two accounts. The first has something to do with the theology of the worshiping community. The episcopal Mass in the cathedral church as described by article 41 of the Constitution on the Sacred Liturgy has a festive character, regardless of the day when it is celebrated. This is presumably true also of the episcopal Mass on a weekday, on the occasion of a pastoral visit to parishes, schools, and other communities. Likewise special weekday "Masses with a Congregation" to celebrate particular aspects of the life of a community are festive. We may include here the ritual Masses and Masses for various occasions such as the seasons of planting and harvesting. The second has to do with the plan of the liturgical year. Weekdays on which solemnities, feasts, and obligatory memorials fall are feast days, although the degree of solemnity will depend on the rank of the feast. Outside of these instances (and probably there are others) the weekday is liturgically "free," and the Mass is ferial.

As regards the shape of the ferial Order of Mass, we can sum up the bits and pieces of information we obtain from medieval sources. Prior to the time when the papal Order of Mass became standard also for weekday celebrations, the ferial must have had an extremely simple format, particularly at the entrance rite. This could have consisted of a greeting, the *Kyrie-Christe eleison* acclamations, a silent pause, and the collect. It is almost certain that the *Alleluia* or tract was not said. There were surely no other formularies for the offertory rite apart from the prayer over the gifts. There would have been no daily commingling with the *fermentum*, though we cannot find out with certainty whether there was also no commingling with the *Sancta*.[28] At any rate, after the seventh century the practice of sending the *fermentum* to the Roman *tituli* was kept only at the Easter Vigil. It would not have made sense to sing the hymn *Agnus Dei* at daily Masses when only one bread had to be broken for a small assembly. This hymn had been introduced in the Roman rite by Pope Sergius I at the end of the seventh century to accompany the lengthy rite of breaking the bread during stational Masses.[29]

Although the Gregorian-Hadrian Sacramentary mentions the embolism to the Lord's Prayer, the greeting (and exchange?) of peace, and the *Agnus Dei*, there is no conclusive evidence that these had been part of the ferial Mass before the stational Order of Mass became standard. It will be remembered that this Sacramentary had originally been prepared for the pope and that the Order of Mass it contains, though usable for presbyteral Masses, had been planned primarily for him.

SHAPING A FERIAL ORDER OF MASS

Preliminary Considerations

The need for a ferial Order of Mass logically follows from the distinction between festive and ferial liturgy. Without progressive solemnity the system of ranking liturgical celebrations falls apart. The very concept of the liturgical year is premised on the distinction between feasts and ordinary days. Since "each day is made holy through the liturgical celebrations of the people of God, especially through the eucharistic sacrifice and the divine office," the degree of solemnity proper to a feast will be reflected by the manner of celebrating the Mass and the liturgy of the hours.[30] Though there is some kind of ferial office and a ferial lectionary, there is strictly no Order of Mass that we can call ferial. Both Sunday and ferial celebrations use the same format, the *forma typica* which is represented by the Sunday "Mass with a Congregation."

When the *Missa normativa* was being prepared, the understanding was that its schema would be the basis for the other forms of the Mass. What are these other forms? According to Cardinal G. Lercaro, these are "Masses for children, for beginners, for the sick." In shaping these other forms "there will be guidelines as to what is to be kept or omitted; in other cases, as to elements in which there is a choice."[31] On the other hand, the Missal of Paul VI distinguishes the forms of celebration according to another system, namely Masses with a congregation, concelebrated Masses, and Masses without a congregation.[32] The General Instruction gives the particulars of each from the entrance to the concluding rite. The variations concentrate on the people who celebrate or on the eventuality of a Mass with only one minister and with no congregation.

Two other forms exist. These are the Masses with special groups and Masses with children.[33] The respective Directories for these special celebrations offer guidelines on adaptations to be made, but these are in connection with the group rather than the day. In other words, these forms of the Mass do not address the question of variations necessitated by the distinction between festive and ferial days. Already during the Council a Father had suggested that "the faculty be granted to vary [the Order of Mass] in the context of the liturgical year."[34]

The present Order of Mass does not of course ignore the distinction between festive and ferial days. The *Gloria* is normally not said at ferial Masses, the lectionary provides only two readings, and the creed is omitted. But that is as far as we are allowed to go. All other variations envisaged by the Order of Mass, especially at the entrance rite, are options that do not touch the question of differentiating the festive from the ferial celebration. Although it would be rather extraordinary, if not odd, to celebrate the daily Mass with all the trappings of a Sunday Mass, no one can stop an overzealous community from executing daily all the provisions of the "Mass with a Congregation." At the other end of the spectrum, we can have the distressing situation of a Sunday Mass celebrated as if it were a weekday Mass.

The ferial Order of Mass should redeem the theology of the liturgical year from the exaggerated notion that one day is as good as the other. This type of egalitarianism can corrode the foundations of the liturgical year. The ferial Order of Mass should display the difference between the ordinary days and Sunday which should stand out more clearly as the Lord's Day, as the original feast of the Christian community. Although in the present theological dispensation the ferial Mass is the center of the daily rhythm of worship, it should be neatly distinguished from the Sunday Mass. The same may be said of solemnities and feasts. Thus the overriding consideration for introducing the ferial Order of Mass is to underline the ritual difference between festive and ferial Masses, between solemn and ordinary celebrations: in short, to apply the principle of progressive solemnity at that level of the liturgical year where the basic distinction is made between Sunday and weekdays.

It is clear then that the concept of the ferial Order of Mass is time-bound. The presence of a large congregation and of a sufficient number of ministers at weekday Masses is not a convincing reason, both liturgical and pastoral, why the celebration should be festive or solemn. In contrast, a small congregation is not a valid motive to strip the Sunday Mass to its essentials. An article published in 1984 gets very close to the idea of the ferial Order of Mass, but its attention is focused on religious communities that regularly celebrate the liturgy of the hours rather than on the distinction between one liturgical day and another. In consideration of the office that precedes or follows the daily eucharist, it would seem to the author of the article that "a greatly simplified rite would be particularly appropriate."[35]

What shape can we envisage for the ferial Order of Mass? It might help allay undue anxieties to premise this with the assurance that an entirely new Order of Mass is not being contemplated here. The *forma typica* presented in the Missal of Paul VI should remain the basic shape on which adaptations for daily celebrations are made. The Directory for Masses with Children sets down the principle: "Apart from adaptations that are necessary because of the children's age, the result should not be entirely special rites, markedly different from the Order of Mass celebrated with a congregation."[36]

To avoid arbitrariness, it would be timely to propose important criteria based on what we are able to gather from liturgical tradition and on the actual *forma typica* of the Order of Mass. First, the format of the "Mass with a Congregation" should be retained. This means that modifications are made within its framework, and that the result is not an entirely new Order of Mass. The aim is not to create something new, but to adapt what exists. Too sharp a contrast between the festive and the ferial Order of Mass would not be pastorally useful in terms of active participation. Biritualism can be very demanding on any congregation. Second, the integral elements of the *forma typica* should be kept intact. Such, for example, is the responsorial psalm, which is "an integral part of the liturgy of the word."[37] Third, as a course of action, it would be advisable not to introduce new rites, acclamations, and responses that are apt to produce a jarring effect on the flow of the celebration and on the assembly itself.[38] Fourth, elements not considered integral parts of the Order of Mass, like the penitential rite, which on occasion is replaced by another rite, and the sign of peace, which is optional, need not be features of the daily Mass. The penitential rite would be more meaningful during Lent. A hard decision will have to be made on whether to keep the acclamations *Kyrie-Christe eleison*. Fifth, it is quite meaningless to retain songs of accompaniment when the action is not fully performed. Such are the entrance song while the priest walks from the sacristy to the altar and the *Agnus Dei* when only one host is broken. The same may be said of a rite that presupposes another rite, namely the washing of hands when no other gifts than bread and wine are presented.[39] Lastly, songs, such as the *Alleluia*, the tract, and the memorial acclamation, which constitute independent rites but are not integral parts of he celebration, are advisedly omitted when they are not sung.[40]

Besides the foregoing criteria, it would be useful to cover briefly what different authors suggest. Though they focus their attention on the question of how the present Order of Mass might be revised in accord with liturgical tradition and contemporary pastoral situation rather than on how a ferial Order of Mass might be shaped, their suggestions are helpful.[41]

As regards the entrance rite, A. Nocent and R. Cabié tend to idealize the early format which consisted of a greeting, silent pause, and the collect. R. Cabié finds the initial sign of the cross "a regrettable alteration," whereas A. Nocent warns against giving too much prominence to the penitential rite. M. Searle seems to favor the sobriety of the entrance rite initially proposed by the study group that prepared the schema of the *Missa normativa*, though he expresses reservations on the quick conclusion of the Mass. T. Krosnicki underlines the ancient use of the *Dominus vobiscum* as a liturgical greeting.

The thinking of F. McManus on the preparation of the gifts merits attention. In line with the *specimen provisorium* prepared by the Consilium in 1964, he would not rule out total silence during the preparation of the gifts if it can support the several ritual acts leading up to the prayer over the gifts and the eucharistic prayer. He suggests reversal to the earliest norms on the prayers to be said privately by the priest: "that the inaudible prayers be left optional, *pro opportunitate*—or simply suppressed entirely." As regards the *berakah* for the bread and cup (two formularies that combine to make a little canon), he thinks that "the simpler and neater solution would be to suppress the two prayers entirely." He favors the opinion that the *Orate, fratres,* which is in fact an overstaying apology in the Roman Missal, should be eliminated in favor of the simple *Oremus* with which the other two presidential prayers are introduced. What F. McManus does seem to suggest is basically a streamlined design for the preparation of the gifts, a design that suits perfectly well the idea of a ferial celebration.

Putting together the various considerations on how the ferial Order of Mass might be shaped, we can envisage concretely a possible format. In any attempt to present a format there will obviously be a number of debatable omissions and inclusions as well as rough edges in the ritual shape. In this connection it might be useful to take two realities into account: first, the existence of the "Mass with a Congregation," which is the basic form of the eucharistic celebration today, and second, the many years of experience people have with Paul VI's Order of Mass, an experience which has acquired the force of habit. The following format relies heavily on these realities. Although it would be preferable to revert to the simple *Oremus* before the prayer over the gifts, this has to wait until the *forma typica* itself shall have been revised. It does not seem convenient to use different formularies for festive and ferial celebrations. Likewise, there are elements in the present Order of Mass that earlier tradition did not know, like the penitential rite and the memorial acclamation. In cases like these, the solution one can adopt is to mark them as optional.

A POSSIBLE SHAPE OF THE FERIAL ORDER OF MASS

INTRODUCTORY RITES

After the people have assembled, the priest and ministers go to the altar. The priest makes the customary signs of reverence and goes to the chair. [If there is no entrance procession, the entrance song is omitted.]

Greeting

After the sign of the cross the priest greets the people with the simple formula: The Lord be with you.

[Penitential Rite]

During Lent the penitential rite may follow, using one of the three forms.

Opening Prayer

Afterwards the priest says: Let us pray. Priest and people observe moments of silence before the priest recites the opening prayer.

LITURGY OF THE WORD

Readings

After the first reading the responsorial psalm is sung or recited. [During Easter season the Alleluia may be sung; if not sung, it is omitted.]

Homily

If there is no homily, a period of silent reflection follows the reading of the gospel.

General Intercessions

After the homily or period of silence the general intercessions, based on the readings, are made.

LITURGY OF THE EUCHARIST

Preparation of the Gifts

The priest prepares the altar and the chalice. In silence he places on the corporal the paten, the ciborium for the communion of the people, and the chalice. [If there is no offertory procession, the song is omitted. If no gifts other than the eucharistic elements are presented the washing of hands may be omitted.]

Then the priest says: Pray, brothers and sisters. . . . The prayer over the gifts follows.

Eucharistic Prayer

The daily singing of the *Sanctus* is recommended. [If the memorial acclamation is not sung, it may be omitted.]

Communion Rite

After the Lord's Prayer and embolism the sign of peace may be given, especially when the occasion calls for it. [If it is omitted, the prayer Lord Jesus Christ and the greeting The peace of the Lord are not said.]

Then in silence the priest breaks the bread. [The *Agnus Dei* is omitted, unless the breaking of bread takes time.] The rite of commingling follows. Afterwards the priest invites the people to communion with the words: This is the Lamb of God. If communion is expected to be protracted, an appropriate song may be sung. After a period of silence the priest recites the prayer after communion.

CONCLUDING RITE

The celebration ends with the usual greeting, blessing, and formulary of dismissal. [The recessional song is not sung.]

Notes

1. *Normae Universales de Anno Liturgico et de Calendario* nos. 17-43, *Missale Romanum*, editio typica altera (Vatican City, 1975) 102-106 (hereafter NUALC); English text in *Documents on the Liturgy*, hereafter DOL (Collegeville, 1982) 1158-1161.

2. Tertullian, *De Baptismo* 9,1, Corpus Christianorum, vol. 1:1 (1954) 8, p. 293.

3. Ibid., 9,2, p. 294.

4. M. Andrieu, ed., *Les Ordines Romani du haut moyen âge*, vol. 2 (Louvain, 1960), pp. 67-108; R. Cabié, *The Eucharist*, vol. 2 of *The Church at Prayer*, ed. A.G. Martimort (Collegeville, 1986) 47-48. See: S. Van Dijk: "The Urban and Papal Rites in the 7th and 8th Century Rome," *Sacris Erudiri* 12 (1961) 411-487; Th. Klauser, *A Short History of the Roman Liturgy* (Oxford, 1979), Chapter 4: "The Roman Bishop's Mass c. AD 700," 59-72; A. Chavasse, "Les célébrations eucharistiques à Rome, V-VIII siècle," *Ecclesia Orans* 7:1 (1990) 69-75. F. McManus writes that "in one sense the eucharist presided over by the bishop is thus the norm and exemplar." "The Roman Order of Mass from 1964 to 1969: The Preparation of the Gifts," in *Shaping English Liturgy* (Washington, D.C., 1990) 112.

5. *Institutio Generalis Missalis Romani*, editio typica altera, *Missale Romanum*, nos. 75-78, pp. 47-48 (hereafter IGRM); DOL 488-489. F. McManus explains that the "Mass with a Congregation, especially on Sunday, "is the exemplar—hence called the *Missa normativa* or later, when this term was misunderstood, the *forma typica*—for all other grades and degrees of lesser and greater solemnity and for all other forms." McManus, "The Roman Order of Mass" 112.

6. A. Bugnini, *The Reform of the Liturgy. 1948-1975* (Collegeville, 1990): "During the Synod Cardinal G. Lercaro pointed out that "there are degrees of solemnity depending on the singing, the number of ministers, and other factors. Thus there can be a Mass of the utmost solemnity that is completely sung, and Masses of lesser solemnity, even to the point of being completely read or recited; in all cases, however, these Masses are distinguished by the presence of a congregation."

7. Ibid. 340-343.

8. IGRM 75, p. 47; DOL 488.

9. Klauser, *Short History of the Western Liturgy* 70. Klauser affirms that there was such a thing as a simple form of the Sunday Mass celebrated by presbyters, but since this was not the normal form not much attention was paid to it.

10. *Bugnini*, The Reform of the Liturgy 349.

11. Ibid. 342.

12. R. Taft, *Beyond East and West: Problems in Liturgical Understanding* (Washington, D.C., 1984): Chapter V, "The Frequency of the Eucharist throughout History" 61-80.

13. A. Blaise, *Lexicon Latinitatis Medii Aevi, Corpus Christianorum. Continuatio Medievalis* (1975) 378-379.

14. NUALC 16, p. 102; DOL 1157.

15. B. Neunheuser, "Le riforme della Liturgia romana. Storia e caratteristiche," *Anamnesis*, vol. 2 (Casale Monferrato, 1978) 240-242.

16. Gregory I, Letter IX, 26, *Monumenta Germaniae Historica*, Epist. 2 (1899) 59; see A. Chavasse, "A Rome, au tournant du Ve siècle, additions et remaniements dans l'Ordinaire de la Messe," *Ecclesia Orans* 5 (1988) 25-44.

17. See Th. Klauser, *A Short History of the Western Liturgy* 34; B. Botte - C. Mohrmann, *L'Ordinaire de la messe: Texte critique, traduction et études*, Etudes liturgiques, vol. 2 (Louvain, 1953); H. Meyer, *Eucharistie*, vol. 4 of *Gottesdienst der Kirche* (Regensburg, 1989) 175. Meyer thinks that the entrance rite in the Roman *tituli* and churches outside the City would have consisted of the litany with the *Kyrie*, silent prayer, and collect. The account given by Augustine of Hippo regarding one Easter Sunday Mass speaks only of a greeting which was immediately followed by the readings. But was it the normal Sunday entrance rite, or had the previous night's vigil or perhaps also the miraculous cure of a young man something to do with its simplicity? *De Civitate Dei* XXII,8, Corpus Christianorum, vol. 48 (1955) 826.

18. J. Deshusses, *Le Sacramentaire grégorien* (Fribourg, 1971) 85-92.

19. See C. Vogel, *Medieval Liturgy: An Introduction to the Sources* (Washington, D.C., 1986) 155-156.

20. Andrieu, ed., *Les Ordines Romani* 115-116. See: A. Chavasse, "Les grands cadres de la célébration à Rome 'in Urbe' et 'extra muros' jusqu'au VIIIe siècle" in his *La liturgie de la ville de Rome du Ve au VIIIe siècle*, Studia Anselmiana, vol. 108 (Rome, 1992) 63-64.

21. C. Mohlberg, ed., *Liber Sacramentorum Romanae Ecclesiae XVIII-XXIII* (Rome, 1981) 189-191; J. Deshusses, ed., *Le Sacramentaire grégorien* XLII-XLVII, 408-411. C. Vogel explains that "in the primitive Gregorian (cf. Had. 202) there was a complete section of *orationes cottidianae* to be

used by celebrants *ad libitum* to compose [Sunday] masses in ordinary time." *Medieval Liturgy*, note 252, p. 129.

22. Andrieu, ed., *Les Ordines Romani*, no. 57, p. 86.

23. C. Molhberg, ed., *Sacramentarium Veronense* XXXII (Rome, 1978) 141. For the question of votive Masses, see S. Marsili, "La prassi celebrativa nell'epoca pretredentina," *Anamnesis*, vol. 3/2 (Casale Monferrato, 1983) 78-89.

24. Mohlberg, ed., *Liber Sacramentorum Romanae Ecclesiae* XXIIII-LXXXIII, 191-224.

25. Deshusses, ed., *Le Sacramentaire grégorien*, LXVIII-XCVI, 431-451.

26. IGMR 329-334, pp. 90-91.

27. J. Jungmann, *The Mass of the Roman Rite* (New York, 1961) 153-168. W. Storey and N. Rasmussen, following A. Häusling, distinguish between "private" and "solitary" Masses. They admit that "private" in the early medieval period "did not refer to something done alone [solitary] but more than likely something 'privated' or deprived of the elaborate or special." *Medieval Liturgy* 156-157.

28. The Order of Mass of the Gregorian Sacramentary includes the *pax* before the *Agnus Dei*. In *Ordo Romanus I* the *pax* was the moment when the first commingling (with the *Sancta*) was done, whereas in *Ordo Romanus II*, the commingling at this point was with the *fermentum*.

29. See Cabié, *The Eucharist* 111-112.

30. NUALC 3, p. 100; DOL 1156.

31. Bugnini, *The Reform of the Liturgy* 353.

32. IGMR 77-231, pp. 47-67; DOL 489-510.

33. Congregation for Divine Worship, *Actio Pastoralis*, *Notitiae* 6 (1970) 50-55; and *Pueros Baptizatos*, *Notitiae* 10 (1974) 5-21.

34. *Schema Constitutionis de Sacra Liturgia*, De Sacrosancto Eucharistiae Mysterio, Modi II, no. 10 (Vatican City, 1963) 8.

35. A. T., "Alternative Forms of Eucharistic Celebrations," *Worship* 58 (1984) 164-167. The author suggests the following format: ritual greeting, readings, silence, prayer over the gifts, eucharistic prayer, Lord's Prayer with its embolism, fraction, invitation to communion, communion, and postcommunion.

36. No. 21; English text in DOL 681.

37. IGMR 36, DOL 478. That is why, "if the psalm after the reading is not sung, it is to be recited."

38. See Directory for Masses with Children, no. 39: "Some rites and texts should never be adapted for children lest the difference between Masses with children and the Masses with adults become too pronounced. These are 'the acclamations and the responses to the priest's greeting', the Lord's Prayer, and the Trinitarian formulary at

the end of the blessing with which the priest concludes the Mass."
DOL 685.

39. F. McManus remarks that "possibly the symbolic washing before
the eucharist begins—or even immediately before the preface of the
anaphora—might have saved it from recent neglect and even
disrepute." "The Roman Order of Mass from 1964 to 1969: The
Preparation of the Gifts" 132.

40. The memorial acclamation is listed among the sung parts of the
Mass. See Congregation for Divine Worship, *Ordo Cantus Missae*
(Vatican City, 1972) no. 14; DOL 1346. As regards the *Alleluia* and the
tract, the norm is they may be omitted when not sung: see General
Instruction 39.

41. A. Bugnini's report on how the Missa normativa was shaped is
basic reading: *The Reform of the Liturgy* 337-392. Enlightening is the
article of F. McManus, "The Roman Order of Mass from 1964 to 1969:
The Preparation of the Gifts" 107-138; see also: T. Krosnicki: "Preparing
the Gifts: Clarifying the Rite," *Worship* 65 (1991) 149-157. Studies and
commentaries on the Missal of Paul VI abound. The folowing are
useful references: Nocent, "Storia della celebrazione dell'eucaristia"
198-270; Cabié, *The Eucharist* 189-220; Meyer, *Eucharistie* 305-392; M.
Searle, "Semper Reformanda: The Opening and Closing Rites of the
Mass," in *Shaping English Liturgy* (Washington, D.C., 1990) 53-92; and
T. Krosnicki, "Grace and Peace: Greeting the Assembly," in *Shaping
English Liturgy* 93-106; E. Foley, K. Hughes, and G. Ostdiek, "The
Preparatory Rites: A Case Study in Liturgical Ecology," *Worship* 67:11
(January 1993) 17-38.

7

Shaping the Filipino
Order of Mass

THE AIM OF THIS PAPER IS TO DESCRIBE THE PROCESS AND THE METHODOL-
ogy that accompanied the work of shaping the Order of Mass for
the Philippines or the *Misa ng Bayang Pilipino*. Basically it is an
attempt to inculturate the 1975 Roman Order of Mass in the
context of the culture and traditions of Filipino Catholics. Its
chief aim is to communicate more fully to the Filipino faithful
the spiritual and doctrinal wealth of the Roman Order of Mass
by re-expressing, through dynamic equivalence, its theological
content. For this reason, the Filipino Order of Mass employs
language, gestures, and symbols derived from the Filipino pattern of thought, speech, and behavior.[1]

It might be useful to preface this presentation with two important remarks. First, the Filipino Order of Mass is not a work
of liturgical creativity, but of a dynamic translation of the Roman Order of Mass. Its point of departure is the Roman Missal
issued by the Holy See with which it conserves substantial unity
in accord with the prescriptions of articles 38, 39, and 63b of the
Constitution on the Sacred Liturgy. Second, the variations in the
plan, language, and rites of the Filipino Order of Mass were
dictated by and large by Filipino religious culture and pastoral
needs.

In conformity with art. 39 of the Constitution, the work of
translating the Roman Order of Mass into the local culture was
guided by the following official documents: the General Instruc-

tion on the Roman Missal, particularly nos. 21, 26, and 56b; the Circular Letter *Eucharistiae Participationem* of 27 April 1973; the Instruction *Comme le prévoit* of 25 January 1969; and the Guidelines *Au cours des derniers mois* of 2 June 1968. And in conformity with art. 23 of the Constitution, the work was carried out, taking into consideration the experiences derived from recent liturgical reforms and indults. These are: the rescript for India regarding adaptations in the Order of Mass, granted by the Consilium on 25 April 25 1969; and the *Missel Romain pour les diocèses du Zaïre*, approved by the Congregation for Divine Worship on 30 April 1988.

The work of shaping the text of the Filipino Order of Mass was guided by the following criteria. First, the texts must clearly express the theological content of the Roman Order of Mass, namely the church's doctrine on the Mass as Christ's paschal sacrifice in the form of a memorial meal which relates to the Last Supper (see SC 47). Second, the texts, which are adapted largely from the Roman Order of Mass, should incorporate genuine Filipino values, idiomatic expressions, proverbs, and images drawn from the life experiences of people. Third, without forgetting the needs of the universal church, the texts should include the contemporary concerns of the church in the Philippines, such as social justice, peace and development, ecumenism, and lay leadership. And fourth, when proclaimed, the texts should be catechetically clear, dignified, and prayerful (see SC 33).

As regards the rites, the following criteria were used. First, the plan of the celebration should be clear, simple, practical, and flowing (see SC 34 and 50). Although it is modelled on the Roman Order of Mass, it should reflect some of the typical Filipino ways or patterns of celebrating a religious event. Second, the rite should provide enough occasions for active and prayerful participation through bodily posture, songs, and responses, and at specified times, also sacred silence (see SC 30-31). And third, the rite should create an atmosphere of prayer and reverence amidst the Filipino pattern of festive or baroque-like celebration.

The inculturation of the Roman Order of Mass started in 1973 as a class project under the direction of this writer at Maryhill School of Theology in the Philippines. In conformity with article 40c of the Constitution on the Sacred Liturgy, the project was presented in the years 1974 and 1975 to a select team of liturgists, theologians, pastors, experts in sociology, cultural anthropology, and linguistics, and officials of the Department of National Language. In 1975 the Episcopal Commission on Liturgy and an ad-hoc committee of bishops made revisions on the proposed text. In July 1976 the Catholic Bishops' Conference unanimously approved that the proposed Order of Mass for the Philippines be submitted for confirmation to the Congregation for Divine Worship. In 1989 the project, which still awaited Vatican approval, was reviewed and emendations were introduced into its plan, rubrics, and language. In July 1991 the Catholic Bishops' Conference accepted the changes and once again requested the approval of the Congregation for Divine Worship.

THE PLAN OF THE FILIPINO ORDER OF MASS

The Filipino Order of Mass follows the Roman plan: introductory rites, liturgy of the word, liturgy of the eucharist (*pagdiriwang ng huling hapunan* or celebration of the Last Supper), and concluding rite.[2]

The following are the components of the introductory rites: entrance procession, veneration of the cross, penitential rite (*pagpapakumbaba* or act of self-abasement), sprinkling with holy water, sign of peace, and the collect. Notable variations have been made in the introductory rites. The presentation of bread and wine as well as the other gifts of the community is done at this time. The rescript for India, no. 10, allowed the same arrangement. Filipinos, like most other people, present their gifts immediately as they come to the place of celebration. The Roman system, on the other hand, joins the presentation of bread and wine to the offertory rite, which is its logical place in the Roman concept of order. Another variation is the inclusion of the veneration of the cross. Filipino Catholics have a great devotion to the cross. Crucifixes are venerated at home or carried about. They make the sign of the cross at every significant moment of their day. The veneration of the cross underlines the theology of the Mass as the sacramental presence of Christ's sacrifice on the cross. The corresponding doxology is a praise of God for the mystery of the cross, on which Christ destroyed death, and of the resurrection by which hope shone on the world. The third variation is the transfer of the sign of peace to this part of the Mass. The sign of peace concludes, as in the Zaïrean Mass, the penitential rite. The rescript for India approved the transfer of the sign of peace also to the entrance rite.[3]

The Filipino plan of the liturgy of the word consists of the following: the veneration of the gospel book, the blessing of the readers, the three readings with the responsorial psalm and gospel acclamation, a song of praise after the gospel reading, the homily, and the general intercessions. Three variations have been introduced into the liturgy of the word. The first is the veneration of the gospel book or, in its absence, the lectionary. The veneration is preceded by an exhortation to honor the holy book and to listen attentively to the word of God. The people respond with a doxology in praise of God whose word reveals the divine will and teaching, and guides us on the path of life. The second is the blessing of the readers. It is part of Filipino religious culture to ask for a priest's or an elder's blessing before performing a special task. This is normally done through the gesture of *mano po*, which consists of taking the priest's or elder's right hand to one's forehead, while the priest or elder says "may God show you his mercy". The gesture signifies respect for authority. The third is the introduction of the posture of kneeling at the general intercessions. Filipinos usually kneel for the prayers of petition. The Roman rite observes this in part at the solemn intercessions on Good Friday.[4]

The Filipino plan of the liturgy of the eucharist follows the Roman model, namely the preparation of the altar and the gifts, though the presentation of the eucharistic gifts is anticipated, the eucharistic prayer, and communion. Three variations may be noted here. The first is the ritualization of the eucharistic prayer. In order to highlight this central and solemn prayer of the church, three forms of ritualization have been added to the rubrics, which every Filipino Catholic would easily associate with solemn prayer: the lighting of altar candles, the ringing of church bells, and the sign of the cross at the start of the prayer. The second is the doxology after the great Amen. Similar doxologies are sung to venerate the cross and the gospel book. There is here an attempt to obtain a sense of balance which is greatly appreciated by Filipinos: the cross is raised at the start and end of the Mass; the gospel book is raised at the start of the liturgy of the word; and the eucharistic species are raised at the end of the eucharistic prayer. The additional doxology, which is sung while the consecrated elements are raised and the church bells are rung festively, corresponds to the Filipino Catholic devotion to the eucharist. It is the assembly's joyful affirmation of faith in the real presence. The third variation concerns the communion of the priest. It is part of Filipino tradition that the head of the family or the host eats last. It is the Filipino way of expressing leadership, hospitality, and parental concern. Incorporated into the Mass, this practice alludes to Matthew 20:26-28.[5]

The concluding rite consists of an exhortation, blessing, and veneration of the cross. The exhortation is called *pagbibilin*, and evokes the reminders parents give to sons and daughters as they take leave. The other variation in this rite is the veneration of the cross. The final doxology, which is sung as the cross is raised, reminds the assembly to live according to the spirit of the eucharistic celebration.

THE LANGUAGE OF THE FILIPINO ORDER OF MASS

The formularies of the Filipino Order of Mass are written in Tagalog. It is the language of several provinces around Manila and was the basis for the formation of the national language called Filipino. Much effort was made, including several consultations with experts in the language, in order to make sure that the formularies, when proclaimed or sung, are clear, dignified, and prayerful.

The language of the formularies for prayer and didascalia is of a literary genre which is slightly poetic, and often observes terminal as well as internal rhyme. The Tagalogs have a predilection for poetic language and for sentences that rhyme, especially for solemn speech. They value rhythmic cadence greatly. For this reason the word order of some sentences had to be rearranged. The formulary of the invitation to the eucharistic prayer will illustrate this.

> *Halina't ipaubaya*
> ang ating mga alalahanin sa Diyos;
> lahát ng papúri at pasasalámat
> *sa kanyá ay áting ihandóg.*

In normal speech the last two lines would normally be arranged thus:

Sa kanyá ay áting ihandóg
ang lahát ng papúri at pasasalámat.

But when proclaimed they lack rhythmic cadence and fall rather flat.

The Filipino Order of Mass employs idiomatic expressions. Idiomatic speech is a sign of how deeply culture has affected liturgical language. Indeed we may say that a person who does not know the idioms of a language does not know that language. Examples of idiomatic expressions in the Filipino Order of Mass abound. At the penitential rite the response of the priest to the request of the assembly for prayer is idiomatic: *ipanatag ninyo ang inyong loob* (literally, "let your innermost being be levelled" or simply "be at ease"). It reassures an anxious person that things are all right. In eucharistic prayer A the phrase *kapos ang aming dila* (literally, "our tongue is short", that is, "words fail us") underlines our inability to praise God sufficiently. In the same prayer the idiom *sinuklian ng kawalang-utang na loob* is used (*sukli* is the change returned for a purchase: "they repaid God with ingratitude").

The Filipino Order of Mass pays special attention to words and phrases which express genuine Filipino values and which can be made to communicate the different messages of the eucharistic celebration. At the penitential rite the value of *hiya* (the attitude that combines humility, unworthiness, and embarrassment) stands out; at the offertory rite *bukas-palad* (literally, "open palms" or generosity) is invoked; at the communion rite the value of *salu-salo* or meal shared among members of the family and intimate friends defines the eucharist as a domestic celebration. Other examples are found in the two eucharistic prayers, e.g.: *utang na loob* (we should show gratitude for God's gifts), *pagsusumikap* (all should work in order to be self-reliant), *pagtitiwala* (God himself was trusting in dealing with humankind), *pakikibalikat* (we should bear with others their troubles), and *pagbabakasakali* (God took a risk when he sent his Son into the world). These words express some of the finest values on human and divine relationship and are deeply rooted in Filipino behavioral pattern.

Sometimes the formularies paraphrase proverbs regarding such Filipino values as generosity, hospitality, dedication to one's duties, and concern for the welfare of others. An example of the use of proverbs is at the time of the collection, when the priest reminds the assembly of a popular saying: *Pinagpapapala ang taos-pusong nag-aalay at bukas-palad na nagbibigay*, meaning, God blesses those who generously give.

A notable trait of the Filipino Order of Mass is its use of dynamic equivalents when it translates key ideas. The purpose of dynamic equivalents is to evoke cultural and traditional rites and paint, as it were, images of a people's life and history. The narration of the institution begins with the solemn phrase *tandang-tanda pa namin* (literally, "we remember very clearly"). The phrase is used to introduce an historical account. By it the storyteller affirms that she or he was present at the event, remembers it vividly, and is thus able to narrate it in great detail. The expression is the church's way of affirming that the church was present at the Last Supper. It is the Tagalog dynamic equivalent for *anamnesis*.

Another key idea is *epiclesis*, which the Filipino Order of Mass renders with the word *lukuban*. This word signifies blessing, care, and protection through the action of overshadowing, and hence can evoke the action of the bird brooding its eggs. Used for the *epiclesis* on both the eucharistic elements and the assembly, *lukuban* expresses the transforming action of the Holy Spirit.

Respect for language pattern and grammatical construction is another trait of the Filipino Order of Mass. In Tagalog the three-fold repetition of a word is considered children's language; used in formal speech it provokes laughter. This is the case with the threefold *Sanctus*. An earlier Tagalog translation rendered it with the Spanish *Santo*. Today, however, *santo* means a saint or an holy image. No one calls God *santo*. The Tagalog word for holy is *banal*, but repeating it three times is linguistically odd. The solution to this problem was to attach a predicate to the word each time it is repeated: "Holy are you, God almighty; holy is your name; holy is your kingdom". The second part, the *Benedictus qui venit*, is contained in the stanza that reads: "We praise and exalt your Son who came to open the eyes of the blind, to make the lame walk, and show compassion for us all." This stanza elaborates the theme of *Benedictus qui venit* by recalling Christ's messianic work.

THE EUCHARISTIC PRAYERS

The Filipino Order of Mass has two eucharistic prayers. The first is slightly longer than the other. When they were composed, attention was given to the Guidelines *Au cours des derniers mois* which deal with the general meaning of the eucharistic anaphora, its essential elements, and the criteria used for the composition of the three new eucharistic prayers in the Roman Missal of 1970. Guidance was also sought from the Circular Letter *Eucharistiae Participationem*.

The Roman Eucharistic Prayers II, III, and IV provided inspiration. The prefaces *pagbubunyi* or exaltation) are inspired by the *postsanctus* of Eucharistic Prayer IV: creation of the world, creation of humankind in the image of God, its infidelity to God, God's response when sending the Son born of the Virgin, and Christ's messianic work. The consecratory and communion *epiclesis* are substantially those presented in Eucharistic Prayers II and III. The reference made by Eucharistic Prayer IV to Christ's "love unto the end" is reflected in Tagalog by the words *nagsasalu-salo sa huling pagkakataon* (literally, "while they were having an intimate meal for the last time"). The memorial oblation of both forms is modelled on Eucharistic Prayers III and IV. Finally the consecratory words and the final doxology are taken from the Tagalog missal approved by the Holy See in 1981 (Prot. CD 915/81). The approval included the new Tagalog version of the *Sanctus*.

The language of the Filipino eucharistic prayers is clear and flowing, and hence is easily accessible to their Tagalog listeners. Care was taken to ensure that the texts are fitted for oral proclamation. It was understood, however, that clarity should not be identified with terseness, stereotyped sentences, and triteness. Hence idioms and proverbs as well as words and phrases that express values are constantly employed in order to produce a colorful and culturally evocative language. Examples of this have been mentioned earlier.

Though largely dependent on the Roman formularies, the Filipino eucharistic prayers differ from them in some aspects. The differences were dictated by the need to foster active participation, meet the faithful's spiritual and devotional needs, and reflect some of the current concerns of the local church like ecumenism, socio-economic inequality, and lay leadership in the church. For this the method of dynamic equivalence was handy. This method was applied to the opening dialogue. The traditional *Sursum corda* and *Gratias agamus with* their responses are dynamically expressed by the priest's words of invitation: "Let us entrust our cares to God, and render him all praise and thanksgiving". The second verse of the doxology sung in response by the people incorporates *Habemus ad Dominum* and *Dignum et iustum est*:

> For it is only right
> that we should all celebrate,
> worship, and give thanks,
> and proclaim and exalt
> his pure, unbounded love.

The compelling reason for this dynamic translation is pastoral, that is, the difficulty to elicit the response of the assembly in short spoken phrases, and the preference the Filipino faithful have for songs.

For greater participation the preface of eucharistic prayer A is divided into three parts. Each part is concluded by one of the three stanzas of the *Sanctus*. On the other hand, the preface of eucharistic prayer B has two parts. For the same reason responses by the people have been added at the intercessions. In order to distinguish this intercessory part of the eucharistic prayer from the general intercessions, the responses are sung as acclamations: "For great is your mercy." And as it has been explained earlier, a doxological song is added to the great Amen as affirmation of the people's faith in Christ's enduring presence in the eucharist.

A WORD ON POPULAR RELIGIOSITY

The Filipino Order of Mass has welcomed expressions of Catholic popular religiosity into its rites and texts. The prominence given to the cross is certainly inspired by the people's devotion to this Christian symbol. The flower petals strewn on the aisle evokes the procession after the blessing of palms on

Palm Sunday. The *mano po* itself is part of popular religious culture. The baroque style of venerating the sacred species at the conclusion of the eucharistic prayer has a strong devotional underpinning.

But the more notable mark of the influence of popular religiosity can be seen in the sung formularies. These are all in stanzas of five lines with eight syllables per line and terminal rhyming. This style of composition was inspired by the devotional book of the *Pasyon*, which narrates in verse form the history of salvation from the creation of the world to the second coming. Its 3,150 rhymed stanzas of five lines each are chanted in a great number of Catholic homes or chapels during Lent. Thus the songs of the Filipino Order of Mass easily appeal to the devotion of the assembly. One practical consideration here is that all these songs can be sung to one of the several tunes of the *Pasyon*.

The following is an example of the *pasyon*-style of composition on which the songs of the Mass have been modelled. It is the first stanza of the book of the *Pasyon*.

O Diyos sa kalangitan,
Hari ng sangkalupaan,
Diyos na walang kapantay,
mabait, lubhang maalam
at puno ng katarungan.

The verse has five lines of eight syllables each. The terminal syllables *an*, *ay*, and *am* rhyme in Tagalog.

ENGLISH TRANSLATION OF THE FILIPINO ORDER OF MASS

The Tagalog text was translated into English by Dom Bernardo Ma. Perez, O.S.B. The translation is not meant for liturgical use but for the purpose of analysis and information. It tries to be as literal as possible in order to capture the linguistic peculiarities of Tagalog. Some idioms simply defy translation, and the rhythmic cadences are impossible to transfer into the English text. In the following text certain Tagalog words and phrases are placed in brackets. They indicate Filipino values and Tagalog idiomatic expressions, proverbs, and rhythmic cadences.

I. INTRODUCTORY RITES

Entrance Procession

Before the procession starts, the commentator introduces the theme of the celebration. The priest, preceded by two candle bearers, the cross bearer, and the deacon or one of the readers carrying the gospel book (or the lectionary), processes toward the sanctuary, while the assembly sings an appropriate entrance song. On solemn occasions flower petals or confetti may be strewn on the aisle.

At the foot of the sanctuary the priest stops to receive from the offerers the bread and wine for the eucharist and the other gifts of the community. The offerers make the *mano po* as they present the gifts to the priest. The gifts are placed on a side table in the sanctuary.

The priest and the ministers bow to the altar; then the priest goes up to the altar and kisses it.

Veneration of the Cross

After the song the priest takes the cross and blesses the people with it, as he chants:

Priest: In the name of the Father,
          and of the Son +,
          and of the Holy Spirit.

People: Amen.

The priest holds the cross aloft, while the people sing:

Let us praise and worship
our Lord and Creator:
the Father who is the source of life,
the Son who is our way,
the Spirit who is our light.

[*Purihin at ipagdangal*
ang ating Poong Maykapal:
Ama na Bukal ng buhay,
Anak na siya nating Daan,
Espiritung ating Tanglaw].

For by the holy cross
of Jesus, our beloved Lord,
death has been overcome;
and at his resurrection
hope has arisen.

Penitential Rite [*Pagpapakumbaba*]

The people kneel. The priest addresses them in these or similar words:

Priest: My brothers and sisters,
with full confidence and with all humility
come before the Lord our God.

People: We want to answer
the summons of the Lord our God,
but we are undeserving and unworthy
[*subalit kami ay alangan
at walang karapatan*].
It is therefore our plea
that you pray for us,
so that the evil we have done
and our failure to do good,
for which we now repent,
may not be a hindrance [*hadlang*]
to our response to his call.

Priest: Take comfort
[*Ipanatag ninyo ang inyong loob*]:
God grants forgiveness
to those who repent for their sins.

The priest sprinkles holy water on the people. They make the sign of the cross.

Sign of Peace

After the sprinkling the people stand. Then the priest addresses them in these or similar words:

Priest: My brothers and sisters,
God has chosen us
and gathered us as one family [*angkan*].

> Let us therefore joyfully give one another
> the sign of fellowship and peace.

The people give the sign of peace to each other according to local custom. The younger ones may make the *mano po* to their elders, while the others may shake hands or offer some other appropriate signs of peace and fellowship.

On solemn occasions the *Gloria* may be sung after the sign of peace. The opening prayer, taken from the sacramentary, concludes the introductory rites.

II. LITURGY OF THE WORD

Veneration of the Sacred Scripture [*Pagpaparangal*]

Priest: My brothers and sisters,
let us honor the Sacred Scripture,
and devoutly listen to the word of God,
that the teaching, which is the light of life,
may be inscribed [*makintal*] in our hearts
and minds.

He holds the gospel book (or the lectionary) aloft, while the people sing:

> Let us praise and worship
> our Lord and Creator:
> the Father who is the source of life,
> the Son who is our way,
> the Spirit who is our light.
>
> For to all the world
> he has revealed
> his will and counsel
> which guide and light
> the path of life.

Readings

The lectors go to the priest and make the *mano po*. The priest hands the lectionary to them, saying:

Priest: As trusted servants of God
[*katiwala ng Diyos*],

be guardians and heralds
of his holy teaching.
In the name of the Father,
and of the Son +,
and of the Holy Spirit.

Readers: Amen.

The priest and the people sit. At the end of the reading the
lector says:

Reader: May this holy teaching
be the guiding light of our life.

After a brief silence, the responsorial psalm is chanted following the arrangement of the lectionary. In special circumstances
the following verse may be sung in place of the responsorial
psalm:

Your teaching and your law
are proclaimed in your word;
and to us is revealed
your gracious will
to save the world.

The second reading follows. After the reading the lector says:

Reader: May this holy teaching
be the guiding light of our life.

After a brief silence the people stand and sing:

Alleluia! Alleluia!
You, O Christ, are our life,
you are our way
leading to salvation.
Alleluia! Alleluia!

During the season of Lent:

Jesus grew in fame:
his goodness and wisdom
were made known to the world;
his pure unbounded love
was made manifest to all.

After the song the deacon or priest reads the gospel. The reader
and people make the sign of the cross on the forehead, lips, and

breast. At the end of the reading the deacon or priest kisses the book and says:

> Priest: May this holy teaching
> be the guiding light of our life.

The people sing:

> We open our hearts
> in praise and thanksgiving,
> for we have been awakened
> to the truth that has been spoken;
> we have been led to the light.

Homily [*Pangaral*]

General Intercessions

For the general intercessions the people kneel.

III. LITURGY OF THE EUCHARIST
[*PAGDIRIWANG NG HULING HAPUNAN*]

Preparation of the Altar and Gifts

The people sit. At the altar the priest addresses them in these or similar words:

> Priest: My brothers and sisters,
> God has deigned
> to make known to us his holy teaching,
> and to gather us around the table of life.
> Let us now joyfully take part
> in the celebration of the Last Supper.

If the collection is to be made at this time, the priest continues:

> Priest: The contributions you give today,
> the fruit of your sweat and toil
> [*na nagmula sa pawis at pagod*],
> will be offered to . . .
>
> My dear brothers and sisters,
> we have been taught
> that God blesses those who give

from the heart with open hands
[*pinagpapala ang taos-pusong nag-aalay
at bukas-palad na nagbibigay*].

The priest prepares the altar and the eucharistic gifts, while the offertory song is sung and the collection is made. On solemn occasions the priest may incense the gifts and the altar.

The priest concludes the rite of preparation with the prayer over the gifts taken from the sacramentary. The people stand for the prayer.

Eucharistic Prayer (Form A)

1. Invitation

After the prayer over the gifts the priest introduces the eucharistic prayer, saying:

Priest: My brothers and sisters,
            let us entrust our cares to God
            and render him all praise and thanksgiving.

The altar candles are lighted and the church bells are rung festively, while the people sing:

Let us praise and worship
our Lord and Creator:
the Father who is the source of life,
the Son who is our way,
the Spirit who is our light.

For it is only right
that we should all celebrate,
worship, and give thanks,
and proclaim and exalt
his pure, unbounded love.

Then the priest and the people make the sign of the cross to indicate that the solemn prayer of the church is about to begin.

Priest: In the name of the Father,
            and of the Son +,
            and of the Holy Spirit.

People: Amen.

2. Preface [*Pagbubunyi*]

With hands extended the priest prays:

Priest: Our Father,
            you alone are worthy of all praise
            and thanksgiving.
            Words fail us
            [*Kapos ang aming dila*],
            when we speak of your power and
            boundless mercy.

            Therefore we glorify you
            who created all things.

The people sing:

            Holy are you, Almighty Father,
            holy is your name,
            holy is your kingdom;
            heaven and earth resound
            with praise for your glory.

            [*Banal ka, Poong Maykapal*
            banal ang iyong pangalan,
            banal ang iyong kaharian;
            langit, lupa'y nagpupugay
            sa iyong kadakilaan].

Priest: You created humans in your image
            and entrusted the world to them.
            But again and again they betrayed you
            [*Muli't muli siyang nagtaksil sa iyo*]:
            your goodness and trust
            they repaid with ingratitude
            [*sinuklian ng kawalang-utang na loob*].

            Merciful Father,
            you did not weary of having compassion
                    for them,
            and of making up for their failings
            [*at nagpuno sa kanyang kakulangan*].
            You even offered [*inalok*] them a covenant:
            they would be your people,
            and you would be their God.

Therefore we praise you
whose mercy is without end.

The people sing:

Father, merciful God,
when you saw mankind,
whom you created and sheltered,
turn against you,
your heart was shaken with pity
[*nabagbag ang iyong loob*].

Priest: Our Father,
at the appointed time
you fulfilled your promise:
you sent your Son, Jesus Christ.
You favored the Virgin Mary,
and blessed her among all women,
so that through the power of the Holy Spirit
she would be the Mother of your only
begotten Son.

Jesus Christ shared the fellowship and
the suffering of every one
[*nakisama at nakiramay sa tao*].
He went about every town to proclaim
his teaching.
He did not hesitate to enter the home of
sinners
[*Hindi siya nag-atubiling makituloy sa bahay*],
and sit at their table
[*at sumalo sa hapag ng taong makasalanan*].

Therefore we praise you
for his teaching and his deeds.

The people sing:

We praise and exalt
your Son who came
to open the eyes of the blind,
to make the lame walk,
and to show compassion for all.

3. Narration of the Institution [*Huling Hapunan*]

After the last song the people kneel. The priest lays his hands on the eucharistic gifts until the words "body and blood of Christ."

Priest: Almighty Father,
           grant us your Holy Spirit
           that he may sanctify and give life
           to these gifts
           [*upang kanyang italaga at lukuban*],
           which will become the body and blood
           of Christ.

           For how clearly we recall
           [*Sapagkat tandang-tanda pa namin*]
           that on the night he was betrayed,
           while he and his disciples were having supper
           for the last time
           [*ay nagsasalu-salo sa huling pagkakataon*],
           he took the bread and gave you thanks;
           he broke the bread,
           gave it to his disciples,
           and said:

           TAKE THIS, ALL OF YOU, AND EAT IT:
           THIS IS MY BODY
           WHICH WILL BE GIVEN UP FOR YOU.

The priest shows the host to the people.

           In the same way, when supper was ended,
           he took the cup.
           Again he gave you thanks,
           he gave the cup to his disciples,
           and said:

           TAKE THIS, ALL OF YOU, AND DRINK
           FROM IT:
           THIS IS THE CUP OF MY BLOOD,
           THE BLOOD OF THE NEW AND
           EVERLASTING COVENANT.
           IT WILL BE SHED FOR YOU AND FOR ALL
           SO THAT SINS MAY BE FORGIVEN.
           DO THIS IN MEMORY OF ME.

The priest shows the chalice to the people.

4. Memorial Oblation

With hands extended the priest continues:

Priest: Almighty Father,
in obedience to the will of Christ
[bilang pagtupad sa habilin ni Kristo],
we now devoutly recall his death and
resurrection,
and as we humbly offer this life-giving
sacrifice,
we wait and eagerly long for his return
[hinihintay at pinananabikan namin].

The priest extends his hands toward the people:

All powerful Father,
grant your Spirit of holiness
to those whom you invite
[inaanyayahan mong sumalo]
to share in the table [hapag] of the
body and blood of your Son.
May your Holy Spirit come upon us
[Kami nawa ay lukuban ng iyong Espiritu],
so that we may become one
in heart, in mind, and in deed
[magkaisa sa puso, diwa at gawa].

5. Intercessions

With hands joined together the priest continues:

Priest: Gracious Father [Amang mapagkalinga],
lead [akayin] your sons and daughters
to perfect unity in faith and baptism,
so that everyone will acknowledge Christ
as the Lord of the universe.
We pray to you.

The last phrase of the petition and the response of the people
are sung:

People: For great is your mercy.

Priest: Guide us, who profess our faith in you,
            especially those who lead and support us
            [*ang mga namumuno at gumagabay sa amin*]:
            N., our Holy Father, N., our bishop,
            all the priests and deacons,
            and the lay leaders who assist the church
            [*ang mga laykong kabalikat ng Simbahan*]
            in her service to your people.
            We pray to you.

People: For great is your mercy.

Priest: Awaken [*imulat*] us to our responsibility
            for one another,
            especially those who suffer,
            the oppressed and the poor
            [*mga sawimpalad, api at dukha*],
            so that we may live our lives
            with diligence and conviction
            [*may pagsusumikap at sariling paninindigan*]
            in accord with your holy will.
            We pray to you.

People: For great is your mercy.

Priest: Grant that we may share [*makasalo*]
            in the blessings of those whom you have favored,
            especially the immaculate Virgin Mary,
            St. Joseph, St. Peter and St. Paul,
            St. Lorenzo Ruiz, St. N.,
            and all the angels and saints.
            We pray to you.

People: For great is your mercy.

Priest: May their fellowship be shared
            by our beloved brothers and sisters,
            who went to their rest, signed with your love
            [*nahimlay taglay ang iyong pag-ibig*],
            especially N.
            Despite their shortcomings
            [*Sa kabila ng kanilang pagkukulang*],
            make them worthy to dwell in your presence.

[*marapatin mong sila'y iyong makapiling*].
We pray to you.

People   For great is your mercy.

6. Concluding Doxology [*Pagpaparangal*]

The people stand. The priest raises the paten and the chalice, chanting:

Priest: Through Christ,
with him,
and in him,
in the unity of the Holy Spirit,
all glory and honor is yours,
Almighty Father,
for ever and ever.

The people sing:

Amen.

The priest keeps the paten and the chalice raised. The church bells are rung festively, while the people sing:

Let us praise and worship
our Lord and Creator:
the Father who is the source of life,
the Son who is our way,
the Spirit who is our light.

For our beloved Lord
showed favor to us, his people;
he did not forsake us
[*at hindi pinabayaan*],
but of his own will
offered us his body and blood.

Eucharistic Prayer (Form B)

1. Dialogue (as in Form A)

2. Preface

Priest: Loving Father,
from the very beginning
you did not regard as strangers
[*hindi mo itinuring na iba*]
the people whom you created,

but instead chose to adopt them,
and in your good ess
you also entrusted to them
all that you have made.

Because of the goodness you have shown,
we cannot remain silent
[hindi kami makapagwawalang-imik];
though our tongues may falter
[maumid man ang dila namin],
we shall still proclaim
how grateful we are to you.

Because of your majesty and power,
we glorify you.

People: Holy are you, Almighty Father,
holy is your name,
holy is your kingdom;
heaven and earth resound
with praise for your glory.

Priest: Merciful Father,
in spite of your goodness
your people betrayed your trust
[nagsamantala sa iyong pagtitiwala],
abandoning the task you gave them
[sariling pananagutan, kanyang tinalikdan].
Nonetheless you took a risk
[Gayun pa ma'y nagbakasakali ka pa rin]:
you sent your only Son, Jesus Christ
our Lord.

In obedience to your will,
he revealed your mercy to all,
and shared the suffering of the poor
and oppressed
[nakiramay siya sa mga api at dukha].

Because of the salvation he brought us,
we praise you.

People: We praise and exalt
your Son who came
to open the eyes of the blind,
to make the lame walk,
and to show compassion for all.

3. Narration of the Institution

Priest: Almighty Father,
           grant us your Holy Spirit
           that he may sanctify and give life to
           these gifts
           [*upang kanyang ibukod-tangi at lukuban*],
           which will become the body and blood
           of Christ.

(The rest as in Form A)

4. Memorial Oblation

Priest: Almighty Father,
           as we offer these holy gifts on the table
           of life,
           we remember your only Son.
           For our sake he suffered and rose again;
           we now eagerly await his return on the
           last day.

           Merciful Father,
           grant that the Holy Spirit be with us,
           that we, who will receive the body and
           blood of Jesus Christ,
           may be gathered and united in mind and
           heart.

5. Intercessions

Priest: Loving Father,
           guide your entire church,
           together with N., our Pope, N., our bishop,
           all the priests and deacons,
           and the lay leaders.
           We pray to you.

People: For great is your mercy.

Priest: Teach us to have compassion
           [*makiramay sa isa't-isa*]
           for the poor and the suffering
           kapus-palad at nadurusa],
           and to faithfully serve the people,
           so that all may share a life of

well-being and prosperity
[upang umunlad ang aming pamumuhay].
We pray to you.

People: For great is your mercy.

Priest: Grant that we may attain your heavenly
blessing [biyayang makalangit]
in the company of the Virgin Mary,
Mother of God,
St. Lorenzo Ruiz, St. N.,
and all who have been faithful to you.
We pray to you.

People: For great is your mercy.

Priest: Remember our departed brothers and sisters,
especially N.
Make them worthy to dwell in your presence.
We pray to you.

People: For great is your mercy.

6. Concluding Doxology (as in Form A)

Communion Rite [Pakikinabang]

1. The Lord's Prayer

The priest introduces the communion rite in these or similar words:

Priest: My brothers and sisters,
come and share in these sacred offerings
[halina't pagsaluhan ang mga haing banal],
that we may be truly united [magkapisan]
in the bountiful feast of life
[sa masaganang hapag ng buhay].

With all confidence
let us pray to our Father in heaven,
as Jesus Christ taught us.

Our Father in heaven . . .
For the kingdom, the power,
and the glory are yours,
now and for ever.
Amen.

At the singing of the Lord's Prayer the people may raise their hands or, according to local custom, join hands with their neighbors.

2. The Breaking of the Bread

The priest raises the chalice, saying:

Priest: My brothers and sisters,
           the cup of blessing which we bless,
           is it not a participation in the blood
           of Christ?

He breaks the bread, saying:

Priest: The bread which we break,
           is it not a participation in the body
           of Christ?

           With humility and trust
           come and share in this sacred offering
           [pagsaluhan ang mga banal na hain].

People: Lord,
           we are unworthy and undeserving
           [alangan at walang karapatan],
           but we commit ourselves
           [sarili'y ipinauubaya]
           to your merciful love.

3. Communion

The communion song is sung. The priest, deacon, and special ministers of communion distribute communion to the people. After the communion of the people the priest distributes communion to the other ministers. He takes communion last. After some moments of silence the prayer after communion, which is taken from the sacramentary, is said.

IV. CONCLUDING RITE

Parting Words [Pagbibilin]

After the concluding prayer announcements may be made. Then the priest addresses the people in these or similar words:

Priest: My brothers and sisters,
as we end this celebration,
I ask you to keep this in mind:
serve your neighbor faithfully,
and let your love bring joy to all
[*ipadama ang wagas na pagmamahal*].

Blessing

Priest: May the blessing of Almighty God,
who guides you in all your ways,
descend upon you.

Then he blesses the people with the cross, chanting:

Priest: In the name of the Father,
and of the Son +,
and of the Holy Spirit.

People: Amen.

Veneration of the Cross [*Pagpaparangal*]

The priest holds the cross aloft, while the people sing:

Let us praise and worship
our Lord and Creator:
the Father who is the source of life,
the Son who is our way,
the Spirit who is our light.

For this is his law
and command to us all:
that we proclaim by word
and manifest by deeds
the love he has revealed.

The priest kisses the altar and, together with the ministers, makes the customary reverence. On returning to the sacristy the priest may pass through the aisle to greet the people.

Notes

1. *Misa ng Bayang Pilipino*, that is, "Mass of the Filipino People." The text sent to Rome bears the title *Roman Order of Mass for the Dioceses in the Philippines*, in accord with the approved *Roman Missal for the Dioceses of Zaire*.

2. The liturgy of the eucharist is called *pagdiriwang ng huling hapunan*, that is, "celebration of the Last Supper".

3. The veneration of the cross, the gospel book, and the consecrated species is called *pagpaparangal*, by which a person is honored or an event is commemorated solemnly and in public. The penitential rite, on the other hand, carries the title *pagpapakumbaba*. This Tagalog word means "self-abasement" more than "sorrow for sins.. It expresses the typical ilipino attitude born of the value of *hiya* (embarrassment, shame, and respect put together).

4. The homily is called *pangaral*, the teaching imparted by parents and elders especially through exhortation. The general intercessions are *pagluhog*. This word suggests prayer of petitions made with humility and fervor.

5. The Tagalog for eucharistic prayer is *panalangin ng pagpupuri at pagpapasalamat*, meaning "prayer of praise and thanksgiving". The word used for preface is *pagbubunyi* or exaltation, solemn praise. The rite of communion is *pakikinabang*, which is traditional among the Tagalogs. It suggests the idea of receiving the "benefits" of the Mass. Although it would have been possible to call the rite *komunyon*, it was felt that the traditional word could be retained because of long usage.

8

Liturgical Pluralism in Multiethnic Communities

ONE OF THE CATCHWORDS THAT HAS BECOME REPRESENTATIVE OF THE program of the Second Vatican Council is pluralism. This word is in direct opposition to uniformity, the word with which the Council of Trent rallied the Catholic Church against Protestant "innovations." The effort of the Tridentine postconciliar reform to bring about uniform observance transformed the liturgy into an unbudging monolith, into a solid monument to the unity of Catholic faith. It produced a liturgy that took no notice of the changes and chances of time, of the ferment of socio-cultural changes that swept across the world, and above all of the changed vision and reality of the local church. With fairness to the Council, which was surely inspired by the Holy Spirit, we should add that it was the best thing that happened to the church at that particularly disturbed moment of its history. The Protestant reform, which was necessitated by the chaotic state into which the church had been plunged by the corruption and decadence of both its leaders and members, did not however bring about pluralism but fragmentation. The Tridentine response to the Protestant "innovations" in the liturgy should be read in the light of this historical reality.

The liturgical reform after the Council of Trent succeeded in instilling the ideal of uniformity in worship. It made absolutely no difference whether the liturgical assembly was composed of tribal communities that inhabited the mountains of Asia and Africa or of the august college of cardinals assisting at a papal

157

Mass in the splendor of St. Peter's basilica. Everywhere the liturgy not only spoke the same language, it also sang the same music. Not a few Catholics gloried in this ideal of uniformity. The liturgists then, or those strict enforcers of liturgical laws, reduced the liturgy to a set of rubrics. The study of liturgy in the seminaries was confined to the correct,valid, and licit performance of liturgical rites. Liturgy meant rubrics.

But uniformity had its price. While it shielded the Catholic faith from the "onslaught of heresy and division," it hid away from the faithful the riches of the liturgy. All too often the liturgy did not nourish fully the spiritual life of the local church. How could it, when its language had been dead for centuries, its rites and symbols were medieval, and its distinctive music, which was the Gregorian chant, belonged to another time and people? This does not mean that the church at that time, the era of the baroque, continued to experience the low ebb. What it means is that the church did not derive its spiritual life principally from the source, which is the liturgy, but from devotional practices. As J. Jungmann has keenly observed, the baroque preferred to draw from secondary sources, which nonetheless nourished an admirable spiritual life.[1] It is the merit of the liturgical movement which flowered in this century to have finally rediscovered the liturgy as the source of spiritual life.[2] Vatican II, as we read in article 10 of the liturgy constitution, had no reservations about describing the liturgy as the fount and summit of the church's life and activities: "From the liturgy, particularly the eucharist, grace is poured forth upon us as from a fountain; the liturgy is the source for achieving in the most effective way possible human sanctification and God's glorification, the end to which all the Church's other activities are directed."

It was a rediscovery in favor of liturgical pluralism. For one, it meant that the doctrinal and spiritual riches of the liturgy needed to be shared with every person in the worshiping assembly and with peoples of every culture and tradition. To bring this about it was felt that the liturgy had to be reexpressed in the language, gestures, and symbols of every local church. And this had far-reaching consequences. The shift from Latin to the vernacular, for example, led to the adoption of liturgical music using contemporary melodies and rhythm, a case perhaps of "new wine in new wineskin"? The problem occurs when the new wine of the liturgical reform is kept in the old wineskin of medieval traditions. The famous "Missa Luba," which was an early attempt to cope with the demands of the reform, is probably an example of putting the old Latin liturgy in the new setting of African music.

WHAT IS LITURGICAL PLURALISM?

At the outset it is important to observe that the process of inculturation begun by Vatican II was motivated from the start by the need to bridge the gap between the liturgy and the living culture of the people. Inculturation was not thought of as a solution to the feeling of ennui and boredom that sometimes comes from the frequent repetition of the same rites, formularies, and songs. There are, of course, people who have an unsatiable thirst for novelty. Inculturation, as the word itself suggests, stems from a cultural necessity, not from a desire for variety, for the sake of variety, or for novelty in the liturgy.

Pluralism is one of the more conspicuous consequences of inculturation. But pluralism, like uniformity, sets its own price. In the church and in the liturgy, changes for good or even ill do not come free. Are we willing to pay the price? If we admit pluralism in our worship, what would happen to the unity of the Catholic Church spread throughout the world, not to mention the central church in the city of Rome? And what about the community life of those parishes and dioceses that are multiracial, multiethnic, multicultural, and multilingual? Would liturgical pluralism not lead to a debilitating fragmentation of these worshiping communities?[3] Pluralism can, of course, imperil that kind of unity which is built on the principle of mere external uniformity. And it can cause immense problems in a parish where the need of ethnic groups to express themselves in their language and native melodies is not duly acknowledged by authority, or where the groups themselves have not learned to respect and appreciate each other's traditions and human gifts. The truth, however, is that pluralism is neither division nor fragmentation: it is a form of diversity within the framework of the one Catholic faith and in the bond of mutual trust, respect, and love.

Liturgical pluralism presupposes the existence of a pluralistic church. Pluralism in community worship will not thrive in local churches where pluralism in membership, structures, and life style is not valued. Several ideas make up the definition of a pluralistic church. First, the members of the ecclesial community come from different ethnic, racial, and social groups. We can form a mental picture of a Sunday assembly composed of people from various races, languages, and socio-economic conditions. An Hispanic sits next to an Asian. The poor are mingled with the wealthy, the children with the adults, and no one feels like a stranger. They all belong; the *domus ecclesiae* is theirs. Second, these various members are allowed and even encouraged to express the faith of the church in the language, rites, and symbols of their traditional culture. Every member of the assembly is grateful for the experience of singing another's native music or answering the greetings in another's language, is delighted to listen to the children's choir, is attentive to the announcement by an employee of a forthcoming strike. Third, the diverse modes of expressing the faith are confined within the bounds of what is considered essential to the basic unity of the church. No one is hurt when told that a certain rite indigenous to one's country of origin or a type of musical rhythm one is used to is not appropriate to the liturgical celebration. Everyone accepts the fact that there are liturgical rules to be observed. This is surely an idealized image of a liturgical assembly, but it describes what is meant by a pluralistic church.

Liturgical pluralism involves the acknowledgement that there are different ethnic, racial, and social groups in the body of the worshiping community. Hence, closing one's eyes to the existence of African-Americans, Hispanics, Asians, and Native Americans offends the universal character of every local church. Article 42 of the Constitution on the Sacred Liturgy reminds us that "the parishes, set up locally under a pastor taking the place of the bishop, are the most important [groupings of the faithful]: in some manner they represent the visible church established throughout the world." The liturgical assembly gathered here and now is the one church of Jesus Christ made up of peoples of every race and nation under heaven. It is founded on the "open-door policy" of the *domus ecclesiae*, a policy whereby all who share the same faith are welcome to join the celebration as full members of the assembly, even if they are strangers to the community. In the final analysis the concept of liturgical pluralism is based on the broader concept of the liturgical assembly as the image and presence of the universal church.[4]

Another component of liturgical pluralism is respect for the dynamism of the culture represented by each ethnic group that constitutes the worshiping assembly. Cultures, like the people that create them, want to be acknowledged and appreciated. In fact, our attitude to a culture is ultimately directed to the group of people who own it. When we ridicule a people's music, we directly or indirectly ridicule the people themselves. It is impossible to speak about cultural traditions in the abstract: there are always humans sustaining them as subjects and agents. This is why, forbidding the liturgical use of cultural expressions proper to ethnic groups, except if they are "indissolubly bound up with superstition and error" or are not "in keeping with the true and authentic spirit of the liturgy," may be considered a measure to stifle the dynamism of culture.[5] Likewise, allowing cultural expressions only grudgingly or allowing their use merely to pacify an ethnic group may be interpreted as ignorance or denial of the inherent value, dignity, and beauty of every culture. One should be wary of courting racial superiority, of falling victim to that distorted sentiment of condescension or pity for other races and cultures that did not produce a Mozart, a Shakespeare, or a Michelangelo. Someone has picturesquely defined pity as the little sister of contempt.

Lastly, liturgical pluralism is built on the principle of unity. Pluralism without unity is fragmentation, just as unity without diversity is domination. The relationship between pluralism and unity will become clearer in the light of a rather technical consideration. We need to deal at this point with two concepts, namely theological content and liturgical form. These two concepts are mutually allied. They are the essential components of each and every liturgical reality. They cannot be separated from each other without injury to the reality they constitute. Thus, the sacrificial nature of the Mass, or its theological content, cannot be separated from its meal shape, or its liturgical form. But while content and form cannot be separated, it does not mean that they cannot be mentally distinguished. One may not pull down a structural column of a building, but one may surely distinguish one from the other.[6]

Unity relates to the theological content, which concerns the meaning and purpose of the liturgy. These must be kept intact despite the differences in cultural expressions adopted by ethnic groups when they celebrate the liturgy. By unity then we mean that across the diversity of languages, musical forms, and symbols, we are able to recognize a particular liturgical celebration as an action of the universal church gathered here and now. Thus the holy eucharist celebrated in the culture and musical tradition of the Hispanics belongs to the Catholic Church, even if its outward shape originates in an ethnic group, even if its cultural expressions are not shared by the Roman rite. Provided the nature and purpose of the eucharistic celebration are kept, we should consider it an action of the church. In short, provided the theological content of the Mass is faithfully kept, it is the Mass celebrated by the church, regardless of its cultural trimmings. The question, of course, and this will be the bone of contention, is whether such a eucharistic celebration is still the liturgy of the Roman rite. Those with a more rubrical and legalistic mind might at most concede validity to it, but they might find difficulty in accepting it as another form of the Roman rite.[7]

Pluralism, on the other hand, refers to the liturgical form or the exterior shape of the celebration. The form of every liturgical rite originates in a particular culture. The meal shape of the eucharist has a Jewish parentage, and so do the sacraments of baptism and anointing of the sick. They have come down to us vested, as it were, in Jewish culture. Our marriage rite, on the other hand, grew in the milieu of the Roman society. It is important to note here that the role of the liturgical form is to render the theological content of the liturgy visible and tangible. It gives body to the content of the rite. But because the liturgical form is by nature and origin something cultural, it can admit variations according to the cultural milieu in which the local church celebrates the liturgy. Whereas the theological content, particularly of the sacraments, requires unity, the liturgical form encourages cultural diversity. We may thus define liturgical pluralism as unity in theological content and diversity in liturgical form.

Having defined the components of liturgical pluralism, we need to ask how it works in multiethnic and multicultural dioceses and parishes. At the outset we should perhaps not lose sight of a contemporary reality that has often bogged down the work of liturgical inculturation. How many nations in the world today can claim to be composed of one race and one culture? The question has a particular relevance for the United States of America which is a rather unique nation.[8] Though it has an indigenous community, it is very much a crossroads of ethnic groups from every region of the world. Its constitutive motto *e pluribus unum* has created the phenomenon of a truly multiethnic nation wherein no single race or culture, not even the indigenous Indian, seems to constitute the substratum of the entire civilization. The Founding Fathers succeeded in carving out political unity from many peoples, *e pluribus unum*, but today there is an ardent interest among ethnic groups to preserve or revive their native traditions and cultural identity, to return to their roots. Such a phenomenon seems to rewrite the venerable motto *e pluribus unum*, so that it would read *in pluribus unum*: unity, not from the confluence of many races and nations, but in the diversity of cultures. The movement toward ethnicity does not seem to pose a political threat, but if it is not guided it can subvert the unity of the Catholic Church. The regrettable experience of the American Church with the breakaway Imani Temple is proof of this.

Nonetheless, if we adhere to the principle of liturgical inculturation, we will arrive at the obvious conclusion that the liturgy should be multiethnic and multicultural. Liturgical inculturation means that in the sight of God and the church all races and ethnic groups are equal. It means that all languages are suitable for the worship of God, that all musical forms, provided they enhance the liturgical rite and text, are welcome, and that all cultural symbols, provided they harmonize with the true and authentic spirit of the liturgy, can be raised to the status of liturgical symbols. In the liturgical farm of the church, to paraphrase a well-known line in G. Orwell's *Animal Farm*, no single ethnic group should claim to be more equal than others.

If pluralism commands a high price, so does the principle of equality. For if every ethnic group has a right to stand before God and worship in the vesture of native culture and traditions, how are we to picture the liturgical life of a multiethnic diocese, let alone a parish? Does it mean that in the same Sunday Mass different languages and musical traditions will be used. Does it mean that there will be different sets of table furnishings and church decor? Does it mean that in the same parish there will be different forms of celebrating marriage, depending on the couple's ethnic allegiance, and perhaps different funeral rites? Will such a plurality of form not strain the forbearance of the parishioners and the pastor himself? All this boils down to one fundamental consideration: are we willing to pay the price of pluralism and equality?

LITURGICAL OPTIONS
FOR MULTIETHNIC CHURCHES

In theory and practice how does liturgical pluralism work in multiethnic communities? What follows is evidently the result of theoretical reflection. This reflection revolves primarily around those dioceses or parishes which take liturgical pluralism to heart and are willing to take a certain amount of risk. For there is no guarantee that every attempt to be liturgically pluralistic will work or is even theoretically feasible. But risk is no reason why new things should not be tried, provided they fall within the confines of doctrinal orthodoxy, liturgical authenticity, and pastoral concern, and provided one accepts the possibility of mistake and has the courage to undo it. On this point the history of the liturgy has much to tell us. A classic example is the cup of milk and honey offered to the neophyte at communion time, between the consecrated bread and the cup of consecrated wine.[9] The paschal symbolism intended by this practice is magnificent, but the risk of misinterpretation on the part of the neophyte and the community as a whole was so great, that eventually the practice was dropped by the churches of Rome and North Africa.

We can consider three options of liturgical pluralism for multiethnic local churches. The first is a liturgy that has the resemblance of a mosaic, that is, a liturgical celebration produced, as it were, by the process of inlaying bits of various cultural traditions in the structure of the rite. For now let us call it *mosaic liturgy*. We can envisage it as a composite liturgy made up of a variety of cultural expressions borrowed from the different ethnic communities belonging to the parish. The Sunday Mass, for example, will be celebrated using the different languages spoken in the parish: prayers in English and readings in Spanish. It will adopt music, gestures, and symbols from the participating groups of Asians, Hispanics, Europeans, and African-Americans. Actually the idea is not new. We know that until the seventh century the Roman liturgy was bilingual, because of the migrants from Eastern Europe. Liturgy values hospitality. Greek *koiné* and Latin were used for the readings on special occasions like Easter and Christmas and for some rites of catechumenate.[10]

Even church architecture and the liturgical furnishings will be influenced harmoniously—let us stress the word "harmoniously"—by native architectural and artistic designs. Thus the *domus ecclesiae* will incorporate the features representing the various ethnic concepts of a home. Viewed from one angle, it will look Asian, from another Hispanic or European. It will surely not look like the traditional gothic or baroque church; it might not even pass for a modern church. What it will represent is not a fixed canon of church architecture, but the image of a multicultural community. It will be built, not with an architectural design as its blueprint, but with the reality of ethnic, racial, and social groups within the community as its model. After all, is not the church building the image of the assembled people? In our case the assembly is composed not of a single race but of a mosaic of races.

Mosaic liturgy is not a novelty nor is it an outrageous one. In fact, its definition fits rather well some of the papal Masses which often give the distinct impression of a cultural crossbreed. However, the option to adopt mosaic liturgy requires an attitude of hospitality and respect vis-à-vis the various ethnic and racial traditions in the same community. It requires the constant awareness that the community is made up of different cultural groups, each with rich and exciting traditions to share. Pope Pius V, the author of the Tridentine Missal, would surely not be able to make out what a mosaic liturgy is all about, but we have no reason to doubt that Pope Paul VI, the author of the Missal of Vatican II, would smile approvingly. The idea of mosaic liturgy is, after all, a logical consequence of Vatican II's Constitution on the Sacred Liturgy (arts. 37-40) which reintroduced liturgical pluralism in the Roman rite.

The second option is a little more difficult to realize. We refer to the introduction of special liturgies that will reflect the cultural patterns and native traditions of each major ethnic group within a parish community: Hispanic, African-American, Filipino, Korean, Vietnamese, and so on. Let us call these special liturgies *pluriethnic liturgies*. Such liturgies presuppose that the diocese or parish can afford the luxury and cost of inculturation. For instance, we can ask whether each ethnic community should have a special place for worship apart from the parish church, perhaps something similar to the idea of national churches, though keeping the parish church as the nucleus of all activities affecting the entire parish community. It is understood that such edifices will be built and liturgically furnished along the traditional architectural design and artistic pattern of each ethnic community. Such an enterprise will surely be expensive and cumbersome even for a wealthy parish. However, we should point out that the architectural design of church buildings, like music and other art forms, is a significant cultural trait of ethnic liturgies.

The option for pluriethnic liturgies carries with it other problems besides the financial burden. One is ecclesiological in nature. What effect will such liturgies have on the ethnic groups' sense for a parish community? Pluriethnic liturgies could become an excuse for the parish community to disintegrate, to be ethnically self-centered. In reality this option is tantamount to the establishment of subparishes. Should it be tried, it would be imperative that adequate measures are taken to ensure that at least on solemn feasts all gather in common liturgical worship, in order to manifest the reality of a single parish community. Pluriethnic liturgies pose another problem which is both liturgical and pastoral in character. Does the parish have available priests who can celebrate the liturgy for each ethnic group? And are there enough liturgical experts in each group to ensure that the liturgy is both in accord with the principles of Vatican II and the requirements of the particular culture?

The third option is simpler to follow, though it will likely be regarded by ethnic groups as less than desirable. Let us call it the *majority liturgy* or a liturgy patterned after the culture and traditions of the major ethnic group in the parish. The idea is certainly an improvement from the situation wherein the liturgy is celebrated exactly as the Roman books describe it, that is, a liturgy which no ethnic group is able to claim as its own. In a sense the Roman model is everybody's and nobody's; it is universal but not local. On the other hand, majority liturgy will focus, for practical more than ideological motive, on one ethnic group, that is, the largest and most consistent component of the parish. The other groups will have to accept the reality of being an ethnic minority, whereas the majority will have to practice the virtue of hospitality. A majority liturgy will probably win favor in democratic societies where the vote of the majority is the vote that counts, but even then the minority has the right to be heard.

These three options are obviously not mutually exclusive. Somewhere along the line they can meet, fuse, or merge to bring about another and possibly more realistic or feasible options. But whichever option one chooses with a view to achieving liturgical pluralism, the basic principle to keep in mind is to preserve the unity of the community in things that are essential. Unity in the church is, after all, the goal toward which the diversity of cultures and traditions should assiduously tend.

HOW INCULTURATION PRESERVES
UNITY IN DIVERSITY

We mentioned earlier that liturgical pluralism is one of the consequences of inculturation. We cannot speak of one without the other. Furthermore, our attitude toward inculturation has necessarily a bearing on our attitude toward pluralism. Faulty ideas and principles on inculturation will produce the wrong kind of pluralism. Sometimes in fact we cannot blame people for their negative or even hostile reaction to liturgical pluralism. Whenever a local church modifies the shape of its liturgical celebration, some people automatically get the unsettling feeling that liturgical tradition is once again being sacrificed on the altar of novelty and innovation. They become uneasy over the fact that there is diversity in the ways and means of worshiping God in community. When several local churches do the same, they begin to wonder what becomes of the unity of the one church spread throughout the world. But when no less than the central church gives blessing to the task of liturgical inculturation, they are confronted by a type of a worldwide diversity whose extent alone boggles the mind.

We are faced here basically with two questions. The first is, how can we ensure that ethnic diversity in the celebration of the parish liturgy will not degenerate into crass individualism and fragmentation? It would indeed be tragic if the liturgy itself should be the cause of division. The second is, what assurance do we have that the changes in the liturgy in favor of an ethnic community truly reflect the culture and traditions of that community? In short, when is diversity another word for genuine pluralism built on unity? Or stated in more technical terms, how does inculturation guarantee the unity of the theological content in the diversity of liturgical forms?

These are the two questions that lead us into the dynamic of liturgical inculturation. At this point it is useful to keep in mind that we are working on the premise that inculturation brings about two realities in the life of the local church, namely: unity in the essentials of the liturgy and pluralism in its cultural expressions. Concretely speaking, unity is guaranteed by recourse to the official liturgical books, while pluralism is achieved by incorporating into the liturgy the cultural patterns of ethnic communities.

Unity in the Essentials of Vatican II's Liturgy

The concept of pluralism allows the shape of the liturgy to assimilate those ethnic expressions which will give to the theological content of the rite a suitable tangible or visible shape. The concept of unity, on the other hand, refers to the preservation of the theological content of the liturgy. In order that pluralism will not become a threat to liturgical unity, it is necessary that the theological content of the liturgy be kept intact. It would be disastrous, if every time an ethnic community works on its liturgy, a totally new and unrecognizable celebration with no link whatsoever to the official worship of the church emerges.

Liturgical inculturation, properly executed, does not produce this type of celebration. The reason is that inculturation is not a work of absolute creativity, even if it is in itself a creative endeavor. It is not absolute creativity, because in the final analysis what it does is translate in a dynamic, that is, cultural, way the content of the Roman liturgy. In other words, inculturation is a means of transmitting unaltered to the people of today the original intent or meaning of the liturgy. It does not create new liturgies in the sense of producing a content other than the one handed down officially by the church. This would not be the scope of inculturation but of creativity. In this sense, a shift in the nature and purpose of a liturgical rite radically modifies its original meaning. It does not mean thereby that the new liturgy emerging from this exercise is necessarily unsuitable. It only means that it exceeds the parameter of inculturation. To those therefore who nurture the suspicion that inculturation is insidious to our liturgical traditions and hence to the unity of the church, we need to give the assurance that there can be no better way to transmit traditions faithfully from one generation to another, while safeguarding essential unity, than by the process of inculturation.

But how does one get to the content of the Roman liturgy or to its basic presuppositions? The answer is, by examining the official liturgical books published by the Holy See after Vatican II. These books, which are called *editio typica* because they are meant to serve as models for the liturgy of local churches, contain what the church has to say regarding the meaning, basic purpose, structural plan, liturgical components, ministers, and other aspects of a particular liturgical celebration. They are published under different titles: the Roman Missal, also called sacramentary, with the gospel book and the lectionary, the Rite of Christian Initiation for Adults, the Rite of Infant Baptism, the Rite of Confirmation, the Rite of Marriage, the Rite of Reconciliation, the Order of Christian Funerals, the Book of Blessings, and so on.

These are the books of Vatican II which the liturgists of each ethnic community should study and consult, even in translation. There they will find suggestions and guidelines on liturgical pluralism. It is not sufficient to study the eucharist and the other sacraments from an historical and dogmatic point of view. They need to examine the official books in order to know which liturgical elements may or may not be subjected to cultural change, if the original meaning and purpose of the liturgical rite are to be preserved. Given the complex nature of these books, it is evident that the process cannot use a shortcut. The chief elements of each rite deserves thorough examination. The liturgists of ethnic communities should have a certain familiarity with the historical background and development of the rite in question. They should apply themselves to a serious study of the doctrine and spirituality of the rite as projected by their formularies, gestures, and symbols. In the words of the Constitution on the Sacred Liturgy, "that sound tradition may be retained and yet the way remain open to legitimate progress, a careful investigation is always to be made into each part of the liturgy to be revised. This investigation should be theological, historical, and pastoral" (art. 23). This is surely a tall order, but there seems to be no other available means to achieve liturgical pluralism in multiethnic churches.

The long and short of it is that if we wish to preserve the essentials and integral elements of Vatican II's worship, we need to examine closely what the official books are saying. The Roman Missal, for instance, informs us of the meaning and purpose of practically every part of the Mass from the entrance song to the rite of dismissal. The General Instruction of the Roman Missal explains that the different components of the entrance rite "have the character of a beginning, introduction, and preparation." It goes on to explain that "the purpose of these rites is that the faithful coming together take on the form of a community and prepare themselves to listen to God's word and celebrate the eucharist properly."[11]

We know from the history of the Mass that the entrance rite has been the most exposed to cultural influences. During the Constantinian era it evolved into an intricate rite that equalled only the ceremonial of the imperial court in splendor. Today in the milieu of multiethnic parishes we observe that the entrance rite usually gets the lion's share in the liturgists' interest and concern. It is clear that such interest and concern will have to be based on what the Instruction says about the nature and purpose of the entrance rite. The liturgists will have to consider the key words and phrases describing the rite: by nature it is a beginning, introduction, preparation; in purpose it forms the liturgical assembly and disposes it to the word and the sacrament. These words need to be analyzed in order to draw the practical consequences for a multiethnic liturgy. All too often we witness entrance rites that try to accommodate every possible cultural element, regardless of whether they fit the rite or not. They are overdone to the point of no longer appearing or serving as introductory rite: they become an independent unit with no visible semiotic link with the principal parts of the Mass.

For an adequate analysis of liturgical texts there is only the hard way, namely the method of textual exegesis and hermeneutics as well as semiotics.[12] This approach might give the impression of intellectual elitism or liturgical exclusivity. Yet we need to give credibility and respectability to the efforts of liturgical pluralism by invoking serious methodology. Multiethnic liturgies are not a child's play. All this leads to the conclusion that, while we should respect expressions of creative spirit and originality, we should encourage the formation of liturgists in the science of liturgics.

Pluralism in Ethnic Expressions

Along with the official liturgical books the culture of the ethnic community has a principal role to play in the development of particular liturgies. In this connection, however, several issues distress liturgists in multicultural churches. Are we able to determine the culture of any given ethnic group, especially when it is part of a multiethnic community and shares several things with other ethnic groups? We might be able to offer an adequate definition of culture, but is this definition applicable to every country in the world today, particularly when the country is a melting pot of different cultures? And lastly, how sure are we that the changes introduced into the liturgy of the parish community in the name of culture and native traditions truly represent the ethnic group?

The good news is that the process toward liturgical pluralism based on cultural diversity does not need to deal directly with these issues. Defining the culture of a people has its value and reward, but it is often nothing more than an exercise in futility, similar to squaring the circle, as far as what we are discussing here is concerned. What definitely helps is the study of the cultural patterns of each ethnic community.

Culture has three principal components, namely values, institutions, and patterns. Values are principles governing the life of a community whether explicitly or implicitly. They shape the social, religious, moral, and political attitudes of the members of the community. Institutions are the traditional rites that celebrate the various aspects of life from birth to funerals, the different seasons of the year, and the cycle of human labor. Cultural patterns, whose concept was developed by Ruth Benedict (1887-1948), are the typical and spontaneous mode of thinking, speaking, and acting common to a particular group. Cultural patterns manifest themselves in the group's social and family traditions, socio-economic activities, and political system. They are innate qualities and are normally shared by members of the group. Thus a person is considered member of an ethnic community, because she or he shares by birth the same cultural patterns. On the other hand, a person who behaves differently from the rest of the community becomes an outcast.[13]

Cultural patterns play a decisive role in the development of ethnic liturgies. When an ethnic community becomes vividly conscious of its cultural patterns, it will react negatively to a liturgy that operates according to a different set of cultural patterns. Thus when the so-called classical Roman liturgy, noted for its sobriety and simplicity, migrated to the Franco-Germanic region after the seventh century, the local liturgists did exactly what they were expected to do. They modified the Roman rite to suit their colorful, dramatic, and vibrant culture.[14] A similar process, thanks to Vatican II, can be witnessed today in several local churches throughout the world because of differences in cultural patterns. It is not far-fetched to predict that for the same reason a plurality of liturgies will eventually emerge in multiethnic communities.

The liturgists of ethnic communities need to focus their attention to cultural patterns, if they wish to develop the liturgy for their respective groups. In the ambit, for example, of the Order of Mass they should be attentive to patterns that can influence the execution of a particular rite. How does the ethnic community express hospitality in words and gestures? How does it welcome its leaders, own members, guests, and strangers? The study of the corresponding cultural patterns will be useful for determining the shape of the entrance rite. Similar questions can be asked regarding the other parts of the Mass, like the offertory rite. Are there specific patterns of words and ritual gestures observed by the ethnic group when gifts are offered and received? Since we are dealing with patterns, it is important to bear in mind the distinction between cultural patterns and institutions or traditional rites. What may suitably be incorporated into the liturgy are not necessarily the institutions themselves, but the pattern of expression and celebration, the way of doing things. The following analogy will help to clarify this point. The inculturation of liturgical music does not consist of fitting texts and formularies to traditional melodies (cf. concept of institutions). Rather, it consists of borrowing musical rhythm and perhaps developing variations on a native musical theme, or in short basing the composition on a rhythm and a theme that characterize the community's musical pattern.

Two concrete examples will illustrate the foregoing discussion. Presumably in line with the Roman cultural pattern of order, the presentation of gifts is done at the beginning of the offertory rite. At first sight it appears to be at its logical place. Where else should it be located but at this part of the celebration? Such an arrangement, however, seems to compartmentalize the Mass and treat its parts like independent units. In other cultural traditions the concept of celebration is one where the parts, flowing from one to the other, are not sharply delineated. Thus, it is quite normal to present gifts at the start of rather than halfway during the celebration. In such a milieu would it not be in keeping with cultural patterns to perform the presentation of gifts at the entrance rite? The other example is the concluding rite, which carries the indecorous name of "rite of dismissal." This part of the Mass, because of its extraordinary brevity and plainness, gives the impression that the people, especially the minister, are in a hurry to leave the church. In many cultures there is a tendency to prolong the ritual of leave-taking. This happens because, out of hospitality, the host dutifully finds excuses to prevent the guest from leaving immediately. Surely the concluding rite of the Roman Mass does not share this cultural pattern.

The long and short of it is that cultural patterns render the development of ethnic liturgies feasible. This approach gives the assurance that the changes we introduce into the liturgy will reflect the culture of the ethnic community, and that it will be able to claim ownership of the liturgy.

* * * * * * * *

In the years following the Second Vatican Council local churches throughout the world have taken truly giant steps to renew liturgical life. The development of liturgical languages, the publication of particular rituals, the active participation of lay men and women in liturgical celebrations and the ministries, the flowering of liturgical music and architecture: all this and more are signs of the "passage of the Holy Spirit in the Church," of a vibrant liturgical life of the Christian people.

But the work has only just begun. Renewal cannot be considered complete until local churches, and we dare say the major ethnic communities, are able to celebrate the liturgy according to their culture and native traditions. In the multiethnic situation of many local churches today, not to mention parishes, inculturated liturgies are another way of saying liturgical pluralism. Perhaps in the final analysis we are dealing here not of an inculturated liturgy for an entire nation, but of inculturated liturgies for each major ethnic group in a parish. In short we are envisioning a plurality of parish liturgical forms based on ethnic traditions. The vision is utopian and the program is rather alarming. Are we willing to pay the price of liturgical pluralism?

In the course of this chapter we outlined what liturgical pluralism means and what it concretely implies. We presented three options for multiethnic communities, namely mosaic liturgy, pluriethnic liturgies, and majority liturgy. Among these mosaic liturgy appears to be the more feasible, given the situation of multiethnic parishes. It also claims an historical precedence. We also allayed the fear of some that such pluralism will injure liturgical tradition and weaken the unity of local churches. Inculturation, which is basically a dynamic translation, ensures that the original message of the official liturgical books is transmitted unaltered, while it allows the culture of the ethnic community to enrich the shape of the celebration. For this reason it is necessary to examine closely the official books issued by the Holy See after Vatican II, since they contain what the church has to say about its worship. As regards culture, we suggested for practical reasons that we concentrate more on cultural patterns rather than on culture itself. In all this there were three overriding considerations: how to interpret the principle of pluralism, how to preserve unity in the essentials of the liturgy, and how to foster legitimate diversity through the assimilation of ethnic expressions.

The signs of the times seem to tell us that the future of the liturgy in multiethnic communities will be greatly influenced by the phenomenon of ethnic revival. Celebrating the liturgy in one parish according to various shapes and styles, allowing a plurality of liturgical forms to suit different ethnic traditions, and having to participate in a liturgy whose language, songs, and symbols belong unmistakably to another culture: such a situation can indeed cause distress. But it is one of the inevitable consequences of admitting the dynamism of culture and the pluralistic nature of the liturgy.

If we accept that the church is universal and that it subsists in ethnic communities, we should expect that the voice it raises in worship will come from every race and nation under heaven. The universal character of the church encourages multiethnic communities to sing to the Lord songs other than ours, songs we have not heard before, songs that are new. In the remarkable words of Pope Paul VI, "the voice of the Church today must not be so constricted that she could not sing a new song, should the inspiration of the Holy Spirit move her to do so."[15]

Notes

1. "Liturgisches Leben im Barock," *Liturgisches Erbe und pastorale Gegenwart* (Innsbruck, 1960) 119.

2. E. Cattaneo credits C. Marmion and L. Beauduin for the realization that the life of faith should be nourished by the richness of the liturgy. *Il culto cristiano in occidente* (Rome, 1978) 587-588.

3. See M. Francis, *Liturgy in a Multicultural Community* (Collegeville, 1991).

4. P. Harnoncourt, *Gesamtkirchliche und teilkirchliche Liturgie* (Freiburg, 1974) 20-59.

5. SC 37. For commentary on SC 37-40, especially the above phrases, see A. Chupungco, *Liturgies of the Future* (New York, 1989) 8-18.

6. For a more detailed treatment of theological content and liturgical form see A. Chupungco, *Liturgies of the Future* 35-40; 71-82 for the

Order of Mass; 125-131 for Christian initiation; 163-172 for the liturgical year.

7. For a more extensive discussion of this topic, see B. Neunheuser, "Servata Substantiali Unitate Ritus Romani," *Ecclesia Orans* 8:1 (1991) 77-95; R. Falsini, "Unità sostanziale del Rito Romano e adattamento," *Liturgia e adattamento* (Rome, 1990) 155-168.

8. Francis, *Liturgy in a Multicultural Community* 39-48.

9. *La Tradition Apostolique de Saint Hippolyte*, ed. B. Botte (Münster, 1989) 21, pp. 54-56.

10. See C. Vogel, *Medieval Liturgy: Introduction to the Sources* (Washington, D.C., 1986) 296-297; for the American scene see M. Francis, *Liturgy in a Multicultural Community* 49-65.

11. GIRM 24; DOL 475.

12. For liturgical hermenutics see M. Augé, "Principi di interpretazione dei testi liturgici," *Anamnesis* (Turin, 1974) 159-179; for liturgical semiotics see A. Terrin, *Leitourgia* (Brescia, 1988).

13. See T. Tentori, *Antropologia culturale* (Rome, 1980); A. Chupungco, *Liturgical Inculturation: Sacramentals, Religiosity, Catechesis* (Collegeville, 1992) 35-37.

14. C. Vogel, "Les motifs de la romanisation du culte sous Pépin et Charlemagne," *Culto cristiano: Politica imperiale carolingia* (Todi, 1979) 17-20.

15. Address to the Members and Periti of the "Consilium" (13 October 1966); DOL 224.

9

Epilogue: History and Culture in the Study of Liturgy

VATICAN II's CONSTITUTION *GAUDIUM ET SPES* MAKES A SIGNIFICANT statement on the role played by culture in the life and mission of the church. In article 58 it declares: "The Church has existed through the centuries in varying circumstances and has utilized the resources of different cultures in her preaching to spread and explain the message of Christ, to examine and understand it more deeply, and to express it more perfectly in the liturgy and in the various aspects of the life of the faithful." In the course of two thousand years the church has been assimilating the cultural resources of every nation in order to evangelize, to theologize, and to celebrate in the liturgy the mystery of its faith. Liturgical history vividly witnesses to this.

The writings of scholars like A. Baumstark, E. Bishop, G. Dix, L. Duchesne, J. Jungmann, and M. Righetti, among several others, drew attention to the cultural underpinning of Christian worship.[1] Thanks to their scholarship the consciousness developed among liturgists that Christian worship, both in its language and rites, is so inextricably bound up with the cultural patterns of nations, that it is not possible to study it, much less celebrate it, outside its cultural context. This cultural consciousness engendered a new approach to the study of liturgy. Liturgical rites and symbols that once upon a time had been interpreted from a purely allegorical perspective began to be explained as historical and cultural realities. The washing of hands at the Roman Mass has nothing to do with the passion story which

177

narrates that Pilate washed his hands; rather it is a residue of the Roman concern for cleanliness. Examples abound and they can be a rather interesting subject of study.

The historical and cultural approach to the liturgy had a strong impact on the shaping of Vatican II's Constitution on the Sacred Liturgy. The Council addressed the issue of liturgical renewal in the light, not only of theology and pastoral concern, but also of culture. Articles 34, 37-40, 50, and the entire chapter on sacraments and sacramentals as well as the chapters on music and liturgical furnishings dwell on the relationship between liturgy and culture. Article 34 is a good example. Although it does not mention the words "Roman culture," it does invoke its patterns when it says: "The rites should be marked by a noble simplicity; they should be short, clear, and unencumbered by useless repetitions." These words are a description of the Roman classical form of the liturgy which assimilated the Roman "genius" for sobriety and practical sense. We come across similar cultural consciousness in practically every typical edition of the liturgical books issued after the Council. The introduction to such books normally contains a section on "adaptation," which often focuses on cultural issues. This is particularly the case with the rites of Christian initiation, marriage, and funerals. On the other hand, the instruction on the translation of liturgical texts underlines the cultural components of the euchological texts.[2] Likewise, the concession to compose new liturgical texts, not excluding the eucharistic prayer, provided they run parallel to those in the typical edition, was surely influenced by the awareness of cultural diversity among local communities.[3]

Article 17 of the Constitution is devoted to the liturgical formation of the clergy. One of the means it proposes is "proper guidance so that they may be able to understand the sacred rites and take part in them wholeheartedly." Genuine understanding of the liturgical rites, each with its history and cultural patterns, is the aim of the study of liturgy. Alas, it happens even today that due to lack of correct historical and cultural perspective the meaning of certain rites is ignored. The entrance song is sung when the presider and ministers are already in their places in the sanctuary. The presider breaks the eucharistic bread and consumes the broken pieces alone. These are some examples of what it means to be insensitive to liturgical history and culture. If we are not attentive to these components of the liturgy, we will treat liturgy as a body of rubrics and discipline.

Article 21 rightly requires that the revision of any part of the liturgy should be preceded by a careful theological, historical, and pastoral investigation. This conciliar norm wishes to safeguard both the doctrinal content and cultural form of the liturgy. To this end the study of liturgy should include due regard for its historical and cultural context. In this way we will be careful not to dismiss too easily the ancient cultural forms of the liturgy on grounds that they belong to another culture and age. Such an iconoclastic attitude can impoverish the theology of the liturgy. We know that many of these ancient forms are rich in doctrine and spirituality. In this way too we will counteract the growing liturgical romanticism and allegorism in some sectors of the postconciliar church. The revival of Latin and Gregorian chant, for example, indicates that some people have not followed the historical process. It is true that articles 36 and 116 of the Constitution, given the peculiar circumstances obtaining in the Council, claim them as distinctive elements of the Roman liturgy. The church of Rome might have delayed the use of the vernacular in the liturgy, but it is part of its tradition to adopt contemporary language in order to foster active participation. To return to Latin as the language of the liturgy, regardless of whether or not the assembly can follow the readings and prayers, is to deny sound tradition and hinder what article 23 calls "legitimate progress."

THE HISTORICAL APPROACH TO
THE STUDY OF LITURGY

Before anything else it might be useful to explain that the study of liturgy has three chief orientations, namely theological, historical, and pastoral. They easily overlap, of course, and are, in any case, mutually inclusive. The theology of the liturgy, which is not exactly the same as liturgical theology, should take into consideration both the historical development of the shape of the liturgy and existing pastoral practice. The aim of history, on the other hand, is to unfold the factors and situations that underlie the development of the theological thinking on the liturgy as well as the church's liturgical discipline. Finally, pastoral liturgy should be based on history, that is to say, in continuity with sound liturgical tradition, and on the solid ground of the theology of the liturgy. Thus these three orientations are so intertwined that the study of one leads to the others. S. Marsili, a foremost liturgical theologian, has summed up this thought in a chapter of a work to which he has given the apt title *Continuità ebraica e novità cristiana*. His theology of the liturgy as a Christian novelty is built on a tradition that goes back to the Hebrew people.[4]

The presence of culture in the liturgy is felt in all areas, and hence it can be a subject of every branch of liturgical study. However, the historical approach to the study of liturgy shows more incisively the interaction between culture and Christian cult. Through the study of history one can verify in both theological thinking and liturgical practice the continuity of tradition. The study of any area of liturgy should thus include its history, not for archeological interest, but for a better understanding of the process of ritual development. We know that the revision of liturgical books after the Council was supported by strong historical data. Now the process of inculturating them presupposes a knowledge of historical development in general as well as what article 23 of the Constitution names "the experience derived from recent liturgical reforms and from indults conceded to various places." In other words, renewal has been launched and should continue to be realized in conjunction with an historical frame of mind. Might it not be the lack of this sense for tradition that has spoiled some attempts to inculturate the liturgy? Might it not be for the same reason that we still witness the tenacity to hold fast to liturgical forms discarded by the conciliar reform, like the Missal of Pius V, especially on the part of conservative movements that challenge the conciliar decision? History is liberating, and those who do not learn from it are indeed "bound to repeat its mistakes."

The study of liturgical history will be immensely beneficial if it is approached from the different cultural epochs in which the church lived. In each of them the church developed its form of worship, especially through textual and ritual creativity which is enshrined in the liturgical books of every cultural epoch. These are the centuries-old witnesses to the influence of cultural patterns and native traditions on the Christian liturgy.[5] M. Augé rightly contends that the cultural ambit, the place, date, and authorship of liturgical texts contained in such books are keys to the correct interpretation of their theological and spiritual message. Exegesis and hermeneutics are, after all, fruitful and beneficial exercises in history.[6] Although it is part of the church's tradition to engage in creativity, it conserves its treasury of liturgical texts with jealousy and pride. The axiom *lex orandi, lex credendi* is just another way of canonizing the euchological formularies contained in liturgical books.

Nonetheless, the student of liturgical history should be equipped with a critical mind vis-à-vis the historical development of the rites. Everything in history has its own justification, though not necessarily its value. Not every text in the liturgical books, not every rite and symbol from the past, and not every feast in the calendar has perennial significance for the life of the church. The reform of the Roman Missal willed by the Constitution (art. 50) eliminated much of the medieval textual and ritual accretions which only served to blur the meaning and purpose of the Mass. Some euchological texts, though venerable in age, had to be modified in order to be more contemporary. The Instruction *Comme le prévoit* admits that "sometimes the meaning of a text can no longer be understood, either because it is contrary to modern Christian ideas (as in *terrena despicere* or *ut inimicos sanctae Ecclesiae humilare digneris*) or because it has less relevance today (as in some phrases intended to combat Arianism) or because it no longer expresses the true original meaning as in some obsolete forms of lenten penance."[7] Certain feasts which belonged to a particular situation in the life of the church had to be either suppressed (this is the case with the finding of the true cross because of its legendary origin) or modified (the feast of Christ the King is now considered the crowning feast of the *anni circulum* rather than a declaration of war against fascism).[8] B. Neunheuser, who accepts L. von Ranke's philosophy that every epoch in world history stands before God, teaches nonetheless that "we have the right and duty to judge whether a [liturgical] form truly corresponds to the demands of the time and the supreme norm of Christian worship."[9]

The student of liturgy should thus know how to critique historical development in the light principally of Vatican II's liturgical principles, like the central position of the paschal mystery, the place of God's word, active participation and all this implies (vernacular, congregational singing, lay ministry), and the ecclesial dimension of the sacraments and sacramentals, among others. These constitute the guiding rule with which to measure whether things are liturgically acceptable or not. The performance of a baroque mass by choir and orchestra that reduces the assembly during Mass to the role of mute audience is surely most unliturgical, though, alas, it is still a practice in some of the revivalist churches. But we should not ignore the many instances of cultural assimilation that have had an enriching effect on the theology and liturgical practice of the church. Some of these, especially those that originate in the Greco-Roman period, continue to adorn the liturgy of initiation. Familiarity with their cultural setting will assist ministers in proposing to the assembly the significance they have for today's world. Sometimes the historical background of rites and symbols, more than the texts that accompany them, can unearth their profound theology. The rite of commingling at Mass, for example, is more adequately explained by its history than by its actual text.

The historical approach is necessary for evaluating and critiquing the actual implementation of Vatican II's liturgical reform. The conciliar principles enumerated above are absolutely solid and should not be too easily subjected to cheap compromises, like the granting of the rather special concession to conservative groups to use the tridentine missal. This missal was in fact the principal object of reform in article 50 of the Constitution. One might call into question the value of Paul VI's Missal, but this does not allow anyone to return to Pius V's Missal, as if article 50 had not been authored by an ecumenical council. The humility to accept an ecumenical council's decision is surely a more salutary attitude than a romantic adherence to the past, however glorious it might have been.[10] Yet this does not mean that everything in the finished product as presented to us by the typical edition of liturgical books is beyond reproach and that nothing more can be done to improve it. In his book *Liturgia Semper Reformanda* A. Nocent offers valuable critique on the typical edition of the Order of Mass, particularly the eucharistic prayer, the lectionary, Christian initiation, and the sacrament of penance.[11] A. Nocent suggests improvements on the basis of these many years of experience with these rites. It is remarkable that in all this his approach has been strongly influenced by liturgical history. Sound tradition, according to the article 23 of the Constitution on the Sacred Liturgy, is the springboard of legitimate progress.

The historical approach is also useful for interpreting correctly the mind of the Council regarding the retrieval of the classical form of the Roman liturgy. This conciliar option is articulated in articles 21, 34, and 50 of the liturgy document. Since the classical form is intimately bound up with the cultural patterns of the Roman people from the fifth to the eighth century, it is historically possible to isolate these patterns from eighth-century accretions of Franco-Germanic provenance.[12] There is no doubt that the *romana sobrietas* and practical sense of this type of liturgy moved the authors of the Constitution to favor its restoration. We are all aware of a number of criticisms regarding this matter. Some consider it an archeological exercise, others a type of scholarly romanticism. We are not in a position to examine here the subjective motive that led to the revival of the classical form. But objectively there is no question that its simplicity and clarity are reasons enough, if active participation is, according to article 14, "the aim to be considered before all else in the reform and promotion of the liturgy." The medieval liturgy, represented by the tridentine books, was too prolix and complicated to encourage active participation. These too are reasons enough, if on the basis of the revised Roman liturgy, as provided for in article 63b of the Constitution, particular rituals are to be prepared for each local church. Without these historical considerations, which are not lacking in pastoral consequences, the Council's adoption of the classical form would indeed be mere archeologism and romanticism.

THE CULTURAL APPROACH TO
THE STUDY OF LITURGY

The other approach to the study of liturgy is cultural. This involves a fair amount of sensitivity to the cultural components of the liturgy as well as to one's own cultural patterns and traditions. A certain familiarity with the notion of culture is a prerequisite to the study of liturgy. From a cultural perspective the liturgy has its own values, cultural patterns, and institutions, just like any cultural group. A brief discussion might help to clarify this matter.[13]

Values are principles that influence and give orientation to the activities of a community; they form the community's attitude toward life and their social, religious, political, and moral behavior. Liturgy also has its values which are parallel to human values, though they are obviously "christianized." Hospitality, for example, is a human value that acquires a profound Christian meaning in the rite of welcoming, together with their parents and godparents, the children to be baptized. Leadership is another value to which the liturgy infuses the Christian principle of ministry and service. The human and Christian qualities of a presider at liturgical celebrations manifest that value.

Cultural patterns are the typical way members of a society think or form concepts, speak, ritualize their life, and express themselves in art. The liturgy too has its own cultural patterns which it assimilated from different cultural groups in the course of centuries. The cultural patterns present in the typical editions of the postconciliar books, though they belong by and large to the Roman classical period, are a conglomeration of various patterns from the Jewish to Christian medieval times. Nonetheless, the Roman liturgy of today has a distinct and typical way of speaking and expressing itself in rites. Its collect formularies, even those recently composed, have a certain literary style and vocabulary that we can call typically "Roman."[14] Similarly, its ritual aspect follows rather strictly a certain typical pattern. Sacramental celebrations are planned with great consistency: introductory rite, liturgy of the word, liturgy of the sacrament, explanatory rites, and conclusion. Songs normally introduce the celebration, greetings are made by the presider at specified moments, silence follows the readings. Because of such patterns the Roman liturgy is highly predictable; it avoids anything that has a jarring effect on the assembly. This again is a cultural pattern originating in the Roman sobriety, symmetry, and order.

Institutions are society's traditional rites which celebrate various phases of life from birth to funeral, the different seasons of the year, and the memorable events in its history. The liturgy has also institutions. It possesses rites to accompany the faithful in moments of crisis, growth, maturity, and life's decline. Sacraments, sacramentals, and blessings are such institutions. The liturgy also celebrates feasts at various times of the year, both solar and liturgical. A number of its feasts were influenced by other religious and secular feasts, like Nativity and Epiphany. Others reflect the different seasons of the year, like Easter and birth of John the Baptist, or perhaps an uneasy political situation, like Christ the King and St. Joseph the Worker on the first of May.[15] But liturgical institutions are Christian institutions: they celebrate the mystery of Christ and his church in the context of people's culture and traditions.

Besides sensitivity to the cultural components of the liturgy, there is need for a profound understanding and appreciation of the people's contemporary language, ritual, and artistic patterns. Liturgists have urgent duties in regard to the relationship between culture and Christian worship. *Gaudium et Spes* (60-62) calls for the recognition of every people's cultural rights and the need to foster cultural education and the proper harmony between culture and Christian formation.

The study of one's own culture is demanded of the liturgical minister whose task is to translate the message of the liturgy in the cultural patterns of the assembly. The message was originally intended for another people in another cultural situation, and it needs to be shared with the assembly gathered here and now. The typical editions of liturgical books always carry options for "adaptation" which the minister may freely make use of in order to foster fuller participation. But such options can be adopted only to the extent that the minister is attentive to the cultural patterns of the assembly. The sad lack of this cultural awareness, and not only the unrestrained enthusiasm for novelty, has often marred liturgical renewal. Liturgical dance, for example, has its rightful place in the celebration, but it can be artificial and rather distracting for an assembly whose religious culture has no place for it during Mass. One could also go to the other extreme by celebrating the liturgy entirely as the typical edition describes it. And since the cultural form of the liturgy in the typical edition often belongs to the classical Roman period, such celebration can be somewhat culturally anachronistic.

* * * * * * * *

After three decades of conciliar renewal the church still experiences a certain division brought about by contrasting ideas of what the liturgy is and how it should be celebrated. Obviously this kind of tension could be a healthy sign that the interest in liturgy has not abated. However, after the Council we are not free to propound our views on what the liturgy is all about outside the principles it has established firmly in the Constitution on the Liturgy. There are surely instances of postconciliar implementation that are at best debatable, but we should be careful to distinguish them from the conciliar principles themselves. To question the validity of conciliar decisions is to challenge the authority of the church. To ignore them, as if they did not exist, is to lack the fundamental trait of loyalty to the church.

The foregoing reflections aimed to pinpoint the causes of a malaise which the postconciliar church has been experiencing in liturgical renewal. There are groups, and their number grows with each passing day, that move with decisive steps toward the rightist view of things. Any change in the liturgy causes them uneasiness, if not outright disenchantment with the reform. Often they find refuge in preconciliar forms which they revive as quickly as they discard the new. In this chapter I have tried to trace the cause. This seems to be, in the final analysis, the absence of an historical and cultural approach to the liturgy or, to put it in other words, a certain inability to combine the two basic concepts of Vatican II's liturgical renewal: sound tradition and legitimate progress. These two are inseparable. Alas among conservatives tradition alone seems to count, and sometimes this is a type of tradition that originated in medieval times. Among some progressives, on the other hand, progress without the backing of tradition appears to be the only means to implement liturgical reform.

Tradition and progress are the two key words which fully express the program of liturgical renewal envisaged by Vatican II. Progress is built on tradition, while tradition sustains and critiques progress. Hence, it is imperative to review history and to learn from it. One lesson we learn from history is that Rome was not built in a day, and that it took almost four hundred years for the Roman Church to develop its own liturgy. The long and short of it is that liturgical renewal requires serious work. We need to engage in the study of liturgy, a study that takes much energy and patience, because it involves historical research as well as cultural awareness. Liturgical renewal is an activity that consumes time and energy, and we cannot use shortcuts to achieve it. A Filipino proverb says that the thorn cuts deep the feet of one who runs too fast. We need to run toward the realization of liturgical renewal outlined for us by the Council, but we should not run as if we did not carry on our shoulders the weight, both heavy and precious, of our tradition.

Notes

1. A. Baumstark, *Liturgie comparée: Principes et méthodes pour l'étude historique des liturgies chrétiennes* (Chevetogne, 1953); E. Bishop, *Liturgica Historica* (Oxford, 1918); O. Casel, *Das christliche Kultmysterium* (Regensburg, 1960); G. Dix, *The Shape of the Liturgy* (London, 1964); L. Duchesne, *Les Origines du culte chrétien: Etudes sur la liturgie latine avant Charlemagne* (Paris, 1925); J. Jungmann, *The Early Liturgy to the Time of Gregory the Great* (London, 1966); M. Righetti, *Manuale di storia liturgica* (Milan-Genoa, 1950, 1953, 1955, 1956).

2. Instruction *Comme le prévoit, Notitiae* 5 (1969) 3-12.

3. Circular Letter *Eucharistiae Participationem, Acta Apostolicae Sedis* 65 (1974) 340-347.

4. S. Marsili, "Dalle origini della Liturgia cristiana alla caratterizzazione rituale," *Anamnesis*, vol. 2 (Casale Monferrato, 1978) 11-39; to some extent A. Adam's *Foundations of Liturgy: An Introduction to Its History and Practice* (Collegeville, 1992) follows this threefold orientation.

5. See, for example, B. Capelle, *Travaux liturgiques de doctrine et d'histoire*, vol. 1 (Louvain, 1955); for an historical and cultural presentation of liturgical books, see C. Vogel, *Medieval Liturgy: An Introduction to the Sources* (Washington, D.C., 1986).

6. M. Augé, "Principi di interpretazione dei testi liturgici," *Anamnesis*, vol. 1 (Turin, 1974) 161-179.

7. English text in *Documents on the Liturgy 1963-1979* (Collegeville, 1982) no. 24, p. 287.

8. For details see A. Chupungco, *Liturgies of the Future* (New York, 1989) 163-220.

9. B. Neunheuser, *Storia della Liturgia attraverso le epoche culturali* (Rome, 1977) 13-14; see also G.-A. Martimort, "L'Histoire et le problème liturgique contemporains," *Mens Concordet Voci* (Tournai, 1983) 177-192.

10. This writer had a chance to observe the tridentine Mass on a Sunday in a parish church. The assembly busied itself with devotional prayers, while the presider and the server "performed" in silence.

11. A. Nocent, *Liturgia Semper Reformanda* (Magnano, 1993).

12. A. Triacca in his article "Tra idealizzazione e realtà: liturgia romana 'pura'?," *Rivista liturgica* 45 (1993) 413-442, asks whether we have not idealized the concept of a "pure" Roman liturgy, and hence embraced a type of "liturgical romanticism." Working on "pure" Roman liturgy, A. Triacca has barked up the wrong tree; he should have considered instead the concept of "classical" Roman liturgy, which is not an idealized concept but a cultural reality.

13. See T. Tentori, *Antropologia culturale* (Rome, 1980); see also: *Liturgie et anthropologie. Conférence Saint-Serge 1989* (Rome, 1990).

14. T. Krosnicki, *Ancient Patterns in Modern Prayer* (Washington, D.C., 1973).

15. E. James, *Seasonal Feasts and Festivals* (New York 1965); Chupungco, *Liturgies of the Future* 163-220; Chupungco, *Shaping the Easter Feast* (Washington, D.C. 1992).

DATE DUE

OCT 2 2 1997			
FEB 2 2 2001			
SEP 0 5 2004			
MAR 1 8 2006			
			Printed in USA